฿ow To Interpret
Dreams, Omens &
Fortune Telling Signs

Fred Gettings

Melvin Powers
Wilshire Book Company

12015 Sherman Road, No. Hollywood, CA 91605

First published and
Copyright © 1967
(Publishers) Ltd.
Greencoat House, Frances Street
London SW 1

Manufactured in the United States of America

ISBN 0-87980-399-1

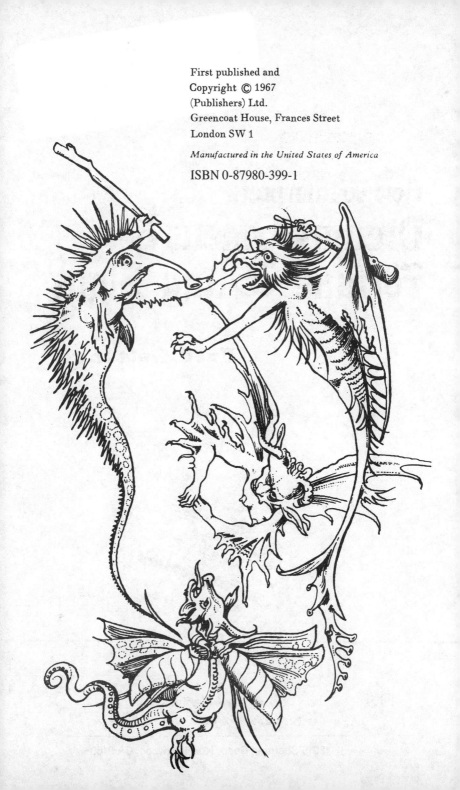

CONTENTS

Introduction

The modern tendency in dream interpretation is to move from a consideration of the isolated symbols to an interpretation of the dream as an organic whole. Whilst the traditional oracles might be inclined to interpret the dream illustrated in terms of FISH or even HAND, a modern interpretation would take into account the whole complex both of the dream situation and the psychological condition of the dreamer. See page 24 where the dream and situation relevant to the illustration is outlined.

From one point of view a dream is a random collection of individual thoughts and feelings which, under the sensory deprivation of the dreaming experience produces for the conscious mind a sequence of bizarre associations, unrelated in regard to time and space. This accounts for the illogicality of dreams, for logic is not applicable since the dream is not directly related to the mind but is more closely connected with the emotions which have their own form of 'logic'. In sleep one part of the mind is deprived of external stimuli and is subject to an almost random series of associations which are noted not as a shadowy interplay of ideas, as in normal thinking, but as 'real' experiences. Anxiety is the chief force which heightens the receptivity of the brain to certain chains of associations, and so there is in fact a degree of selectivity which gives rise to the apparently 'random' selection of data in a dream. In the example illustrated it is the anxiety concerning the daughter which actually sparked off the chain of 'illogical' associations involving the child.

"THE PIG DREAMS OF ACORNS, THE GOOSE OF MAIZE", runs the Hungarian proverb, politely expressing the idea that a dream is always completely egotistical. We dream always about ourselves, and a dream is really nothing more than a stage presentation in which no costs are spared—the actors and the properties and the theatre with only one person in the audience, the dreamer himself. In the dream all ones different personalities, possessions, hopes and fears, are symbolised in one way or another in a fictitious setting, and it is the business of dream interpretation to find out what this nightly play—be it comedy, tragedy or farce—means to the dreamer.

It has been suggested by modern psychologists that a dream is an attempt on the part of the subconscious to tell the dreamer something in a way which is acceptable to him. The fact that so many dreams are obscure or prevaricate or talk in innuendoes is simply because a great deal of what the subconscious mind wants to say is quite unacceptable to the conscious mind. A dream is very often a 'polite way of putting over a truth', and the part of our mind which manufactures dreams (that is, allows the subconscious to communicate with the conscious mind) stands as a kind of sentinel to make sure that the various home truths and bits of unpleasant information are not so shockingly obvious or hurtful as to wake the dreamer. When the message is particularly strong, it sometimes presses past the sentinel and wakes the dreamer: very often such dreams are called nightmares!

Thus, the dream is a sort of guardian of sleep as well as a means of communication between the two halves of man which are usually separated in waking life. One way in which the dream acts as a messenger, and at the same time preserves sleep, is by means of symbols. The symbols disguise the truth, be it pleasant or unpleasant, and the fantasies into which the symbols are woven entertain the mind in sleep. An example of the way in which symbols are incorporated into dreams may be taken as follows. Supposing the subconscious mind (which, for the sake of saving argument, we assume knows more about the personality and his role in life than the conscious mind) wants to tell the dreamer that he is not giving his daughter enough attention in the right way, and she is suffering because of this. The subconscious cannot pass the message on in a direct way, for the man would not listen, or could not listen, because it would upset his pride. In any case the dream sentinel will not allow the conscious mind to come out with such a thing in simple terms for it would disturb the dreamers' sleep. *The beans cannot be spilled, so to speak, so they must first be canned and neatly labelled. The dreamer will only see the can or the label, but the beans are still in the can, and the dream interpreter has a good strong can opener* — provided, of course, the dreamer really wants the truth. Supposing the dream sentinel allows the subconscious to pass on its message in the following dream:

You are sitting by a fresh stream when a beautiful fish swims near to the surface, almost as if it wants to speak to you, but it cannot speak because it is only a fish. You bend down to stroke it, and as you touch its back it leaps out of the water. It lies on the path, gasping for breath, and you watch it, rooted to the spot. The fish wriggles and gasps, and you are afraid it is going to die, but you cannot help it for you are unable to move.

Now it would not be very difficult for someone with an elementary knowledge of dream symbolism to see what the 'message' is in this particular dream —provided, of course, that he knew something about the background of the dreamer himself. Although the dream sentinel has disguised the message of the subconscious in order that the dreamer may remain asleep, he has not distorted the intentions of the subconscious, with the result that on walking the dream may be scrutinized in order for the sleeper to gain some idea of what he must do to. preserve his inner balance—which is the aim of such communications as this. The dream interpretation might run:

A stream is recognised as a persistant symbol of the source of life, and it is often related to the mother and wife. From this comes a fish, which is very often a symbol of a girl child. There is some division between the dreamer and his wife, for the fish leaps out of the water to be with the father. The dreamer wants the child, and the child wants the dreamer (it leaps out of the water – that is out of its natural setting—as soon as the dreamer reaches to touch it) but it is not easy to communicate since the dreamer and the fish belong to different elements. It is clear that the child is not receiving the right sort of attention, for it is quite literally, 'a fish out of water'—and the dreamer cannot or will not help it. The fact that he is rooted to the spot and cannot put the fish back into the water may be interpreted as a desire to help the child being frustrated by a fear of failure due to some personal childhood experience (this is a common explanation of the dream of 'being rooted to the spot'). The dream as a whole appears to be a warning that the dreamer must face up to his present fear and make some attempt to help the child with the right sort of attention, otherwise she will not grow up properly. The difficulty in the fish 'breathing' suggests incorrect organic functioning or an incorrect environment—both of which are the responsibility of the parent, the dreamer.

In such a way the dream interpretation opens the can and pours out the beans—which may well be more 'edible' during waking hours.

You will note that within the interpretation each of the dream symbols was related to something relevant to the dreamer himself—a fish in the dream of another person might well have meant something else — yet there is an underlying sense and structure in the dream as a whole when seen in the light of such an interpretation.

No-one has ever been able to lay down a strict code of dream interpretations, though men have been trying to do so for many thousands of years. All attempts to strictly tabulate a symbol to one meaning is bound for failure, and this is why the common dream oracles, which are so often tightly fixed arrangements of symbols and meanings, are of little value in dream interpretation. Actually, this kind of static dream interpretation from fixed symbols is almost certainly a direct result of the invention of printing! It is only since the fifteenth century that fixed dream oracles have become so popular. It is apparent from the records which have survived from long before this time that the early dream interpreters were rather like the modern psychologists and tended to treat the dreams brought to them in terms of the background and general psyche of the dreamer himself, and it is unlikely that the now popular fixed symbols were established in the early times. When publishers started producing 'dream books' the mediating role of the interpreter was lost, and the books followed an in the dubious mediaeval tradition that each symbol in a dream should have one fixed meaning. As a result of this almost every dream book produced, even in modern times, consists of an alphabetical list of words with hard and fast dream 'meanings' which may be attached to the dream symbol, irrespective of the background or emotional state of the dreamer:

FISH Catching fish—*you will be loved very much.*
Dead fish—*expect trouble.*
Cooking fish—*marriage.*

and so on. Such fixed interpretations which have grown into 'dream oracles' are on the whole very disappointing, for they do not relate to anything specific to the dreamer; they are not particularly interesting as interpretations, and there is no background of 'logic' in the way the symbols are presented. In other words, they are not systems of interpreting dreams. There are, however, two very interesting developments behind the way the majority of such oracles are presented.

In these dream oracles almost all dreams which are obviously sexual in quality are either ignored in interpretation or are afforded 'meanings' which are banal and rather obviously invented and unreal

11

—almost as if the erotic element in a dream is a quite distasteful thing. *For example:*

SEDUCE	Being seduced – *will have plenty of money.* Seducing a woman by force – *good events to come.*
SEXUAL ORGANS	Exposing sexual organs – *danger.* A woman having unusual sexual organs – *children will have a good reputation.*

Along similar lines, a dream of intercourse may be interpreted as a sorrowful event, a dream of a bride as a childless marriage, a dream of adultery as a fire, and thus the whole matter of sex in dreams is reduced to trivial nonsense!

On the other hand, one finds very many erotic and sexual interpretations afforded to fairly trivial dream symbols, so that a dream of a full moon means that you will be seduced, a dream of a peach means that you will be reunited in love, and (significant in itself) a dream of a pile of rubble means a coming marriage for the dreamer. A dream of a seal coming out of the sea means that the dreamer (apparently irrespective of sex) will become pregnant!

This sort of inversion of a dream for interpretation—the translating of a sexual dream into a trivial meaning, and the transposing of a trivial symbol into a sexual significance—is one of the favourite tricks of the dream sentinel. Inversion is his most common device, *so that a thing in a dream is very often least what it appears to be.* This fact was well known to the earliest dream interpreters, many modern psychologists, among them Freud and Stekel, have also observed its importance in dream interpretation.

However, inversion is not a rule which can be applied to all dreams, and very often the only real meaning which can be applied to a symbol must spring from the dreamer himself when he is analysing his dream. This is the 'psychological method' whereby the talking about a dream to another person very often reveals the real meaning of the dream to the dreamer. It must be remarked in passing, however, that the strict symbol system of the common oracles is by no means restricted to books—very many interpreters, including Freud who should really have known better, have tried to formulate a system of symbols and meanings with obviously absurd results. Stekel, for example, suggests that anything which can fly is, in a dream, a symbol of death!

We must remember that just as there is much confusion and disagreement in traditional dream oracles as to the significance of certain dreams, there is much the same disagreement with psychologists. Freud would see a serpent as a sexual symbol—very possibly as a phallus—whilst Jung would see it as a symbol of healing, relating it to the ancient medical symbol, whilst Stekel would side a little with Freud and see it as a symbol of the volvula. The interpretation of 'serpent dreams' in the records of psychology differ widely, and often appear to be contradictory until related to the case history of the dreamer himself. But, such difference apart, if we pay attention to the earliest interpreters we find a striking resemblence between what people like Artemidorus and Ibn Sirin saw in certain recurrent symbols and the way they are interpreted by modern psychologists such as Freud, Jung and Stekel.

Jung, who has himself done so much for modern dream interpretation, admits quite candidly in one famous passage that he has no theory about dreams, and explains that although he has little faith in traditional oracles, because of their arbitrariness, he is none the less convinced that dreams do have a meaning. He says, 'if we meditate on a dream sufficiently long and thoroughly—if we take it about with us and turn it over and over—something almost always comes of it', for he is certain that a dream is a practical way in which the subconscious may inform the dreamer where he is going in both a psychological and *physiological* sense.

Since it is only commonsense to put aside the old rigid system of symbol interpretation, we are faced with interpreting each dream as the organic thing it is, without reference to strict symbols. Fortunately, there is a whole body of agreement between ancient and modern sources as to the general meanings of certain kinds of dreams, and this body of material is incorporated into this book. Where traditional oracles either support or throw light on the basic material they also are accomodated, for not only are many of them interesting and amusing, they often tend to spark off the intuition into an understanding of the dream itself.

Although it is clear that rule-of-thumb interpretations should be avoided where possible, it does not mean that we should reject as useless the whole body of traditional material, for experience shows that correctly understood, this is of considerable value in dream interpretation. Accordingly, several of the fixed traditional interpretations are included in the text, in indented paragraphs and related to the less static interpretations afforded to their class by modern psychological ideas.

The text has been written so as to be read as a whole, and it is interspersed with records of relevant and amusing superstitions which are of interest. From the text it should be possible for the reader to interpret the dreams he has in a whole rather than as a system of uncoordinated dream fragments. One must try to take into account the framework of the dream, its setting, the obvious individual symbols and their qualifying conditions, before attempting to relate these to ones own experience. If we take the example dream from page 11 we should note that the main conditions were that we found ourselves by a stream; the fish came out of the water willingly; and we experienced the fright of not being able to move to help it. A clue to the meaning of this dream would have been gained by looking up STREAM, FISH and PARALYSIS, and relating these to the background of the dreamer himself.

INDEX

LA·LUNE

THE BODY
in dreams

The 'nudity' dream (see page 23) illustrates the need to take into consideration the circumstances of the dreamer when interpreting a particular dream. The meaning of a dream such as the one illustrated will depend on at least two important factors—the sex of the dreamer, and the emotions accompanying the dream. If the dreamer is female, then it may well be that the dream is an expression of a desire to act out her own exhibitionism, and the fact that this particular dream is enacted in an escalator, with all the associations of the 'bra and pantie' adverts, suggests that the dreamer may well be saying to the world (and to herself): "Look, I've got a better body than these models have!" The importance of such a dream would have to be related to the background of the dreamer, for it could be involved with a fear of her own sexuality, which indicates a need to restore self confidence. Such considerations can only be determined by examining the emotions which accompany the dream. A feeling of liberation (emphasised by the fact that this nude woman is ascending a staircase) will indicate the wish to restore self confidence, whilst a feeling of guilt will relate to sexual fears. A male dreamer involved in the situation depicted may very probably be participating in what Freud termed 'wish fulfilment'; though very few dreams may be interpreted quite so simply.

1 IN dream interpretation it is most usual for the various parts of the human body to be identified with people who are related in some way with the dreamer himself. The head, for example, is seen as the figure of authority—most usually the father; whilst the eyes are identified with the dreamer's children, and so on. Thus a dream in which any particular organ of the body receives emphasis must be interpreted in terms of the traditional significance of that organ. A further system of correspondencies is seen in the identification of the body with the home of the dreamer, in which the head is related to the roof, the feet to the foundations, the stomach body in the dream must therefore be regarded as affecting the corresponding parts of the dreamer's house or home. Springing from such a traditional background we have a typical oracle which reads

> To dream of one's own home being old and dilapidated means the death of a close relative is at hand.

> A dream of a house being torn down is a warning to prepare for sad news concerning yourself.

2 Stekel, the modern dream interpreter, points out that in a dream the nine orifices of the body are regarded as interchangeable—so that a dream of an ear may, for example, refer to the anus. This is one of the most common ways in which 'the dream stands sentinel over our sheep' (see page 10 of the Introduction). Perhaps the dream oracles hint at this with the traditional interpretation:

> If a woman dreams that one of her ears are being stopped up it means that she will be the victim of much gossip.

3 A dream of human flesh, especially that of the dreamer himself, is always a dream of personal belongings, and usually presages an increase in possessions. A dream of eating human flesh is especially a sign of coming riches. From Artemidorus to Freud such a dream has always been interpreted as the appropriations (by fair means or foul) of another person's property — for flesh is a symbol of money and belongings, and the act of eating is clearly the act of assimilating into one's own body. Artemidorus tells the story of the man who had three sons and dreamed that two of them had burned and eaten him. The youngest remonstrated with them, saying that he would not and indeed could not eat his father. As might be expected, the youngest son died, and was not able to share in the fortune of his father. This Artemidorus was able to predict from the man's dream.

A dream of your own fingernails indicates a **4** dispute ahead, whilst a dream of someone cutting your nails indicates dishonour in the family. The nails are obviously a symbol of the self, of something very personal, and even in the earliest Egyptian dream books we find that to dream of having one's nails torn out is interpreted as a loss of all one's property (literally: 'all that one has in one's hands'.) A dream of long nails indicates riches to come, short nails, discord. The identification of nails with the special 'essence' of the person has been used to great effect in witchcraft and black magic spells, thus:

> Pliny saith that the parings of a sick man's nails off his feet and hands mixed with wax, cure fevers if they be fastened to another man's gate before

the rising of the sun. Fevers may also be cured by binding the parings of the nails of a sick person to the neck of a live eel in a linen cloth, and the eei be let go into the water.

5 Teeth in dreams also relate to something valuable in the life of the dreamer. In view of this it is not surprising that a dream of loosing one's teeth is almost always interpreted as the impending loss of something valuable, and particularly as the loss of one's parents. There are several interesting stories which have survived in dream oracles concerning dreams of teeth. Perhaps the most celebrated is the one about the Arabian Calif who dreamed that his teeth dropped out. An oneiromancer was called and he duly interpreted that the dream was a bad omen meaning that the Calif's parents were shortly to die. The Calif was not amused and had the dream interpreter whipped. Another oneiromancer was called, and this one, clearly *au fait* with the fate of his predecessor, interpreted that the dream was a good omen meaning that the Calif was going to outlive his parents. The Calif was relieved and overjoyed. After rewarding the interpreter he remarked that although the two meanings were obviously the same, the latter had been formulated in a much more acceptable manner. In modern times
6 Stekel tells of a dream which one of his patients had. In the dream his false teeth fell out and three of the teeth were broken. The patient, Stekel informs us, at the time suspected his wife's fidelity and was not particulary happy at home, in spite of his love for his two children. Stekel interpreted the dream as an expression of his patient's wish to escape the

married state, for the false teeth represented his false wife, and the breaking of the three teeth symbolised the death of his wife and two children —which would alone free him of his responsibilities and worries. Thus we see that in ancient and modern dream interpretation, the loss of teeth is connected with death or with the death wish. There is much divergence, however, between modern interpretation and the traditional oracles concerning other 'teeth conditions':

A dream of a tooth growing inwards means **7** forthcoming news of death, and brushing the teeth of children indicates that you will need to borrow money from near relatives. A dream of brushing your own teeth means misery ahead, and a dream of gold teeth indicates a state of unhappiness.

Modern psychologists have interpreted the dream of teeth falling out as a sign from the subconscious that the dreamer should 'grow up in life' (accept responsibilities which he or she is shirking) because of the obvious link with the loss of the milk teeth which marked a stage of growing from infancy to childhood.

There is a tradition in folklore that a child born **8** with a tooth in its head will be unlucky, violent or have a real temper. Christina Hole records a modern midwife in Oxfordshire still believing that a child with a tooth in its mouth at birth will grow up to be a murderer! It is interesting to note that in the days when teeth extraction was a little better than barbarous there existed a whole body of magic spells for removing teeth which had decayed or were painful. Here is one:

> Take wormes when they be a gendering together; dry them upon a hott tyle stone, then make a powder of them, and what tooth ye touch with it will fall out.

9 The tendency in ordinary life to identify the presence of much hair with virility and strength is projected into dreams, in which hair is regarded as a symbol of the vital force. Thus, to dream of long hair indicates that riches, dignity and power are ahead for the one who has the hair, whilst a dream of short hair, or even worse of having one's hair cut short, indicates poverty and dishonour around the corner. The theme of Samson and Delilah probably has its origin in early dream oracles. An Arab book of dreams recounts the story of a man in Baghdad who dreamed that he had his hair and beard shaved off, and who received an interpretation from a well known oneiromancer that this indicated that he would loose his goods and reputation. In order to avoid his fate the man remained indoors for a few days, and yet, no sooner had he stepped outside than he saw an acquaintance being taken to the scaffold. The friend publically accused him of being implicated in his crime, and the unfortunate man was taken and beaten before being thrown into prison for a long time. "Have you ever heard of such an exact interpretation as that one?", the man asked his listeners afterwards, perhaps a little ruefully. The way in which the hair grows, the colour of the hair, and what is being done to it, is of considerable importance in the interpretation:

A dream of red hair means you are telling lies.
A dream of having a crew cut means you are
being cheated.
A dream of brushing your own hair means that
you will be very short of money soon.

A dream of hair growing on the back of the hands **10**
means financial gain, and this oracle probably has
its origin in the northern belief that such hair in
real life indicates that the person will become rich
in life. The folklore belief that one loses one's hair
and become bald through worry is linked with the
idea of personal belongings and property being
identified with such personal characteristics as hair
and teeth and finger nails.

To dream of hair growing on the edge of the **11**
mouth indicates a sudden death. To dream of
white hair means dignity, blond hair friendship,
and black hair means that the dreamer will be
involved in a car accident. To dream that your
hair is turning white means that you will be
separated from dear ones. A dream of burning
hair means that a friend is going to die, and a
dream of having your hair combed indicates the
beginning of a new friendship.

In the oldest dream oracles the eyes represent the **12**
sons or daughters of the dreamer, and so a dream of
becoming blind presages the death of one's own
child. This interpretation appears to have been a
result of the similarity of sound in the greek word
for 'pupil' (of the eye) and 'girl', yet the interpretation has persisted even into modern times.
Certainly the eye is something precious, and may

well be identified in dreams with one's most precious effects. The various interpretations afforded the eye in a dream revolves around this idea of 'valued possessions', and is a good example of the subconscious use of direct symbolism (see page 9 of the Introduction). To dream of being worried about your eyes, for example, means that you have to be careful about what you are doing. A typical 'inversion' is the interpretation of a dream in which you are admiring your wife's eyes—this means that you will be unfaithful to your wife. Curiously enough, however, for a wife to dream of admiring her husband's eyes indicates that a baby is on the way. The colour of the eyes seen in the dream is of considerable importance, so that whilst black eyes mean misery and red eyes mean illness, blue eyes mean joy.

26

If you lose your eyes in a dream, decay of circumstances, death of a dear friend, disappointment in love; if you get new eyes, or more than you ought to have, shows increase of family.

To dream of a beard is really to dream of hair in **13** excess (see page 29) with all the associations of success and sexual virility.

For a pregnant women to dream of a man with a beard means that she will give birth to a son. A girl dreaming of a man with a beard indicates that she will marry the one she loves. To dream of losing a beard, or of being shaven, means financial ruin. An excessive long beard in a dream presages a downfall or illness.

The tendency in modern interpretation is to regard the beard as a phallic symbol, so that a patient who

The dream illustrates how a variety of interpretations may be attached to one relatively simple dream complex. Orifices are interchangeable in dreams, and this may be taken as an example of dream inversion (see page 33). Although the dream of a man issuing from the mouth may be interpreted in terms of a strictly sexual context it is a fairly simple dream to remember and ponder—it is presented in a way which is quite acceptable to the conscious mind. Cannibalism is related to the idea of a person assimilating the body of another person, and by natural extension the dream of being eaten or of eating someone is related to sex and love. Such a dream may be connected with hostility—for example the female is 'devouring' the male by oral aggression, and at the same time she is presenting the male in her dream as being very much smaller (and therefore inferior) to herself. From another point of view we may see this dream in terms of 'possession' —the idea that a person may be possessed by evil spirits—by opening the mouth the girl is actually getting rid of (perhaps spitting out) and rejecting the man who 'possesses' her in the mediaeval sense of the word —and thus the whole dream is to be interpreted as a wish fulfilment to be rid of the man in her life—in this case her husband!

dreams of having his beard or moustache off may well be expressing an urge to be rid of his penis (a wish to become a woman?) and to avoid certain kinds of responsibility. Traditional interpretations do not avoid the sexual significance, and it is held that for a pregnant women to dream that she herself has a beard means an abortion, whilst for an unmarried woman to dream of having a beard means gambling losses, and for a married woman to dream similarly means divorce (which is a king of gambling loss!). For a young girl to dream of a small beard means that matrimony is on the way.

The belief that the vital force of the possessor was found in the beard was so well established during the middle ages that certain kinds of contracts were sealed with hairs from the beard—a kind of sympathetic magic.

If you dream you are brushing your hair it portends riches and success in love.
To dream that you have wool instead of hair foretells (according to Artemidorus) that you will have long sickness, and fantasies and toe-itch.

14 The interpretation of the meaning of urine in dreams has varied a great deal, so that in one traditional oracle a dream of urinating simply means that one will have to sweep the floor—a fairly certain prophecy! Other oracles suggest a close affinity between urine and sperm, both for the male and female dreamer, thus suggesting that urine betokens creative power and strength. Such an interpretation was obviously accorded to the dream of the daughter of Astygates who saw herself inundating the whole of Europe with her urine. The magicians who interpreted her dream said that this meant that her son would rule over the whole of Europe—the name of her son was Cyrus. The more commonplace traditional oracles make much less sense, obviously avoiding the issue:

> To dream of wetting the bed means a good outcome to business affairs, and to dream of children urinating means that the dreamer will have good health.

It is believed in many parts of Britian that if a person should be bewitched, the spell can be broken by boiling the person's urine to which nail parings had been added. This had to be done late at night in a sealed room.

Chilblains are cured by massaging the hands or feet of the patient in his own urine whilst it is still warm—thus showing the identification of urine with strength and healing powers, as seen in dreams.

> An acient cure for bed-wetting is to have the child make water on the grave of a child of opposite sex.

This cure, like the threat of the Miceman, presumably works on the fear principle.

In dreams the blood is a powerful force which is **15** often interpreted as the soul or money of the dreamer, and what is happening to the blood must be interpreted accordingly—loosing blood means sickness (literally: "weakening of the spirit"), whilst the sign of clothing stained with blood means that your affairs in life will be hampered and restricted by others. As for Macbeth, blood on the hands betokens evil to come—though it is usually interpreted as relating to love affairs only if the blood should be on the dreamer's hands. Blood transfusions in dreams break away from the tradition, for although the dream of giving a transfusion certainly implies a loss, receiving a transfusion means the achievement of ones desires. A dream of a sick man being donated blood implies shame ahead for the dreamer.

More than all other 'personal possessions' represented by the parts of the body, the blood is regarded as the vital force of the person or animal. It is because of this that the ancient ritual of blood drinking has persisted for so long—the practice is based on the belief that by drinking blood one is able to assimilate into one's own system the strength and spirit of the person. This was certainly the idea of those soldiers who drank the blood of the executed duke of Montmorency in 1632, in an attempt to pass his bravery into their own bodies. On this belief is founded also the idea that a pact with the devil must be signed in blood, and that 'blood brothers' must exchange each others blood into their veins. The custom of launching a ship after breaking a bottle of champagne over her bows is linked with blood sacrifices. In ancient times important ships were launched over human beings, so that their blood spurted over the stern and keel as it went onto the waters. In certain parts of the world, even today, animal sacrifices are made in a similar way—the blood being 'offered' to the ship as a propitiation to the gods. Such connexions as these have, of course, entered into black and white magic. One curious spell which survived well into the last century reads:

For a maid wishes to see her lover, let her take the following method. Prick the third or wedding finger of your left hand with a sharp needle (beware of a pin) and with the blood write your own and lovers name on a piece of clean white paper, in as small a compass as you are able and encompass it with three rings of the same crimson stream. Fold it up, and exactly at the ninth hour of the evening, bring it with your own hands in the earth, and tell no one. Your lover will come to you as soon as possible, and he will not be able to rest until he sees you, or if you have quarrelled, to make it up. A young man may also try this charm, only instead of the wedding finger, let him pierce his left thumb

The general tenor of dreams of the body can probably be gathered from the above records. The following traditional readings will help with other organs and bodily parts, before we deal with the fairly common dream of being nude.

16

Artemidorus says that a dream of a great head is good for a rich man who hath not as yet any great estate or dignity. A dream of a cut finger shows you will have a law suit about money already paid.

For to dream you have ox horns, or any such like violent beast, fortels violent death, and chiefly beheading; it being incident to horned beasts, saith Artemedorus.

To dream of having feet dislocated means an illness in the family soon.

To dream of a broken foot means the loss of a relative by death.

17 There is a certain degree of similarity in the various interprctations accorded to the common dream of nudity. The underlying belief is that the dream of being naked in the presence of others who are clothed is an attempt of the subconscious mind to say to the dreamer, "you are not what you try to pretend to be", councelling a change in behaviour. It is generally held that the shame which attends such a dream is not so much a shame of nudity so much as a shame of being 'found out'—the personality does not want to stop pretending. In popular dream interpretation there is a distinct link with this idea, for a man seeing himself naked in a dream must interpret it as meaning that a closely held secret will be be revealed to all and sundry. A woman seeing herself exposcd in public has an even more distressing fate for she will become a prostitute!

For a dreamer to see another nude is a bad sign —a naked woman means the death of someone, whilst a naked man means public distress.

A dream in which one sees oneself naked in a **18** crowd, with no particular feeling of shame, may be interpreted by a modern psychologist as an exhibitionist dream or as an expression of a need te be more frank in life—both these propensities being repressed in waking life. Jung sees such dreams as means of restoring self-confidence, for the dreamer is seeing quite clearly that no-one minds what she is really like (symbolising her regrettable personality passing unnoticed).

A nineteenth century oracle poem on the dream of nudity runs:

> This omen's no good, 'tis with scandal propense,
> And argues a habit to envy intense,
> To see women naked sad whimsies obtrudes,
> Which clothes not your back, nor affords you sound foods;
> Tho' still some old women abstinaciously prate you,
> That some unexpected high honours await you.

PEOPLE

This particular dream is a good example of the subconscious mind attempting to inform the conscious mind about some pressing element in the general psyche which is in need of attention. As we have already noted (see page 41), the unknown person in the dream is almost always the dreamer himself; the actions of the unknown person are usually such that the dreamer would not openly wish to associate with them consciously. In this case we see that the dreamer does not wish to identify with his own aggressive feelings which are symbolised by a man operating a machine gun. 'Repressed aggresion is often related to deprivation in childhood, and consequently a dream of this type may be interpreted as a warning from the subconscious that the dreamer should attempt to be more assertive in life, and to recognise that his general timidity (which is affecting his survival) springs from his own deprived childhood, and this should be recognised. Thus we see an example where a difficulty in facing up to a problem in life may be overcome in a dream, for in the dream one need not immediately identify with the enactments presented to the conscious mind.

41

19 IN dreams the majority of the people—the actors—may be identified, and their identity qualifies the meaning which may be attributed to their appearance in the dream. However, there is one type of dream which is by no means uncommon—that of an 'unknown' person who can sometimes not be clearly distinguished and at other times appears to be a complete stranger. Such a dream is often very revealing, for with it the sentinel of sleep is often lacking in his duties. Freud has already pointed out that dreams are completely egoistical, and infers that an unknown person in a dream must surely be the dreamer himself 'in diguise'. Obviously, the nature of the disguise will lend a clue to the particular problem of the dreamer, and if this 'unknown person' is doing something which the dreamer himself would consider reprehensible, then he can be sure that it is not merely wishfulfilment which initiated the dream!

Some oracles, and indeed some psychologists, have occasion to interpret the 'unknown man' as an image of death who is seeking to abduct the dreamer or the others in the dream. To a certain extent the general agreement about this symbol supports the idea that all unknown and unrecognised elements in a dream symbolize hostile forces. This is precisely why a name is so important—it serves to identify and therefore render 'known' the element in the dream. Primitive tribes (and indeed many civilized beings) regard a name or a word as having a magic power, and it is believed that if one knows the name of something or someone then one has power over them. There are many related interpretations in the traditional oracles, all connoting hostility because of the 'unnamed' quality of the personage. Armed people mean that you will be attacked or arrested, blind people bring real misfortune, and even uninvited guests bring tears in the future. It is certain that if the person in your dream cannot be identified, then it must be interpreted as a hostile sign—if he can be identified then the significance of his appearance will depend on his nature. A woman in a dream is usually an image of the *anima* of the male dream, the 'true love' who will mingle with his *animus* and make him a complete being. According to Artemidorus, however, an old woman is a symbol of death. If a female dreams of an unknown woman this means great difficulties ahead, for the woman must be a rival or enemy. On a psychological level, this is a dream of the shadow—the objectionable side of the dreamer which is usually hidden behind the personality.

For a woman to dream she is courted by an old **20** man is a sure prognostication that she will receive a sum of money. For a maid to dream of it, shows that she will marry a rich young fellow, and will have many children by him, who will all become rich. For a man to dream he is courting an old woman and that she returns his love is a very fortunate omen and denotes success in worldly affairs, that he will marry a beautiful young woman, have *lovely* children and live happily.

In no other field of dream interpretation are the two **21** camps of traditional oracles and modern psychological work so divided and opposed as in the matter of parents. There can be no doubt that on a psychological level a dream of the father is a sexual dream. The common dream of the death of one's father is accordingly seen as a wish fulfilment by some psychologists, and is therefore considered a favourable release. The traditional oracles tend to identify the father in dreams with the father in life, and so a dream of the death of one's own father is interpreted as a catastrophe ahead, and a lack of success in business. It is more realistic, however, to interprete a 'death of father' dream in terms of the particular circumstances: in some instances the dream is surely the inner self warning the person that he is ignoring his father, perhaps not listening to his advice, perhaps not paying him enough attention, suggesting in strong dream images that the father 'just might as well be dead for all you are concerned'. To dream of talking to father is a sign of happiness, yet paradoxically, to dream that father is poor means that all one's desires will be accomplished. It is interesting to note that men dream more frequently of the death of their father, whilst women dream more frequently of the death of their mother. This has been interpreted as a result of jealousy—the son seeing in his father an potential rival, the daughter seeing such a rival in her mother. Like the dream of the father, the appearance of the mother is full of sexual significance, and Stekel has actually gone so far as to identify the dream mother with the uterus. The dream oracles in the traditional vein are less precise and a good deal more humanitarian, and so we find that a dream of living with one's own mother is merely a wish for security, but a dream of your mother being dead means that your property will be in danger. To see your mother pay you a visit in a dream, whilst you are actually away means that you will be returning home quite soon.

To dream you're a mother foretells some good news, or letters from friends.

The self is usually easily identified in the dream as **22** either the chief personality in the dream (remember that a dream is purely egotistical, for it is a play written by one person for only one person to witness!) or he is the 'unknown' person who for some reason is hiding his identity. The dream of coming face to face with oneself is an expression of a need to examine one's conduct in the light of its effects on one's own inner balance. The traditional symbol for coming 'face to face' with oneself is the looking glass dream:

> These incentives to vanity troubles engender,
> And construe some fraud to the feminine gender.
> To the wife they portend many children and grief,
> And from her relations but little relief;
> But when a fond maid, self in glass shall survey,
> She is then, I pronounce, in the family way.

Death dreams fall into two categories; there is the **23** dream of someone dying or being dead (including the dreamer) and there is the dream of meeting Death, either in the form of a skeleton or an 'unknown' person whom you take to be Death himself. The interpretation of both these 'death dreams' vary enormously. On the whole, however, it is worth noting that a dream of being dead oneself does not presage death but, curiously enough, happiness. For example the Talmud says that for a dreamer to see a dead man in his own house always means that there will be peace in that house. However, it must be observed that there have been many records of people dreaming of deaths and their own deaths prior to the event and being proved right. An this way Abraham Lincoln saw himself in his coffin a few days before his death, and heard someone in his dream explain that the President had been assassinated. One of the most famous of the death dream cases is that of the eighteenth century French actor Champmesle, who dreamed that his deceased mother and wife appeared to him and his mother beckoned to him. He told his friends of the dream, paid for a funeral mass for himself and after hearing it sung he left the church and whilst talking to some friends outside he dropped dead. Although Freud tends to think of the death dream as occasioning prophetic warning, some psychologists interprete such dreams as expressing a strong desire to live more fully. In this interpretation they echo the traditional oracles, which nearly always interpret death dreams in fortunate terms

> A dream of the death of a pregnant woman means that a fortune will be received from abroad, and a dream of helping to bury dead people means success over present enemies. A dream of a person being dead who is really alive means loss in legal matters, and the reverse dream implies sorrow in the family.

24 In spite of President Lincoln's dream (recorded above), a vision of a dead person in a coffin is usually interpreted by the oracles as nothing less than a prophecy of indigestion! However, some dream books do suggest that under certain circumstances the appearance of the figure of a dead man in a dream betokens death. If one dreams of death in a sick man's house, then it means that the man himself will die. If one should dream that one marches closely behind the figure of death, this also means that one will die, and if a man dreams that he is being dragged into a church or some such place, it signifies that he will die a lingering death. To kiss a dead man suggests that illness is on the way.

A captain of the cosacks tells a story of how whilst he was on the Turkish front during the 1915 campaigns he found a hanging man and had him buried. That night he dreamed that the man came to him and warned him that he would be ordered to make a patrol in a certain direction and this would certainly lead to much danger. Accordingly, he managed to secure a command of a different patrol next morning. The captain who headed his original patrol was severely wounded and many of his men were lost.

A dream of a lover   25

> If he kiss you 'tis bad, but his flatt'ry is worse,
> As he'll prove when husband both stern and morose;
> Tho'should he e'en strike you, no matter, his worth,
> His affection, will balance the stigma of birth.

And finally, the dream of children: 26

> Should a female, who's not in the family way,
> Dream of having a child, 'tis most lucky, they say;
> But if she's a maid, let her prudence advance,
> Or her chastity stands but a very bad chance.

The two examples of nightmares illustrated on pages 49 and 65 demonstrate how fear is the root of such 'dreams'. In the first dream we see fear of the inevitability of decay and death, and in the second dream we see a fear of the loss of identity in the technocracy of the twentieth century. Such kinds of dreams are always related to the feeling that the self is in danger of being annihilated.

In the dream of monsters, aged people, and the hanging man we see fears transplanted into various forms connected with senile and posthumous decay—and the dream may be related either to fears of age and death or to ones own impulses to self-destruction. An ambivalent relationship may give rise to dreams of this kind, or a situation in which one is being organically or emotionally restricted, for the frustration of impeded development calls into question the whole repertoire of thoughts and emotions concerning the purpose of the individual and the inevitable end.

NIGHTMARES
and bad dreams

27 No one is quite sure what a nightmare means or how it is caused, but more than other dreams they tend to be repeated, and they are usually such that even if the dreamer cannot remember the details of the nightmare, he will almost certainly remember the fear which accompanied it for a considerable time afterwards. In this connexion psychologists have shown that nightmares, like ordinary dreams, may colour the whole day in an individual's life with foreboding and apprehension, and thus affect even his major decisions during that day. Explanations for nightmares vary a great deal—from the ancient explanation that they are caused by a succubus (a devil in human form) lying with the man or woman and having intercourse in order to give birth to evil spirits, to the modern explanation which suggests that they are based on repressed sexual desires, such as desire for incest! Traditional dream oracles tend to skip over the problem of nightmares, and treat the individual creatures seen in such dreams (like crabs, spiders and vampires, which Jung sees as typical archtypes of the nightmare) as symbols in the normal way, often reversing the frightening images into beneficient predictions in a not very convincing way. Thus, tradition has it that a crab in a dream means a new lover; a spider means much happiness on the way, and a vampire means that you will marry for money.

Artemidorus relates that all monsters are impossible, and mean vain hopes of things which shall not fall out.

To dream of seeing a giant is ominous of good; if you are in trade you will have good increase of business from foreign parts.

It is certain, however, that there is something different about a nightmare, and the images have an insistence and clarity which lift them well clear of such pedestrian interpretations. Clearly, fear and anxiety are the roots of nightmares, and it is for this reason that they afford such a clue to the psychological interpreters—to such an extent that one psychologist can write that with the aid of a nightmare it is possible to see the real trouble which is the root of the patient's difficulties, whilst with ordinary dreams it is possible to find some solution to the problem.

The monsters and vampires we see in dreams are the personification of our emotions of rage, fear and sexual desire, and for this reason the interpretation must be made in terms of the individual rather in terms of strict symbol interpretation. Certainly we must reject the traditional oracles which claim that a nightmare is 'a sign of treachery from someone you trust', for a thing so vivid and violent as a nightmare must surely mean more than that! Nightmares fall roughly into two broad divisions—one in which the dreamer is menaced by monsters or recognisable creatures such as spiders or werewolves, and the other in which the dreamer is not menaced by anything, but is in some difficult or frightening situation, such as being rooted to the spot or falling, or being unable to breath. Sometimes, of course, these two forms of nightmare combine, when for example one dreams of being rooted to a spot by oozing mud, with a savage giant bearing down on one. Whatever the individual interpretations of such nightmares, we see that the traditional dream books are often at great variance with the modern psychological interpretations which tend to see nightmares. like certain kinds of 'death dream' as emotional summaries of repressions in the dreamer.

Thus, a traditional interpretation of a monster in a dream is that there are good times ahead, though should the monster be in the sea one might expect reverses, and the common nightmare of being pursued by a monster means that sorrow and misfortune will certainly overwhelm you! A fairly typical psychological interpretation of such a nightmare would be that it was an expression in symbolic form of an inner emotional conflict: the monster is an incarnation of desires or emotions which frighten the dreamer, even though they are an integral part of his psyche. Such a dream might well relate to a desire for incest with the mother, though it must be noted that the modern tendency is to relate each nightmare to the particular case history of the dreamer. In closer contact with the traditional oracles, certain psychologists maintain that nightmares, like 'death dreams' are actually emotional summaries of the dreamer's state of mind, and they have a tendency to regard such a typical nightmare as seeing ones teeth falling out as an expression of an urgent need to grow up—perhaps to accept certain responsibilities—expressed symbolically as a memory of the move from infancy to childhood which was a growing stage marked with the milestones of fallen teeth.

28 Fairly typical traditional dream book interpretations follow—

This awful phenomenon inculcates to all,
The fate that to man must infallibly fall.

Then remember to die, is the bold way to face it,
Nor care you how soon then is sculptur'd 'Hic Jacet'.
To dream of the dead proves the visits of strangers,
After absence of years and escape from dangers;
But seeing relations or friends with the dead,
Is a sign of much sickness, their death, it is said.

The common enough nightmare of being rooted to the spot, or being unable to run away quickly enough, whilst being menaced by monsters, witches, dragons and the like, is linked by modern psychologists to insecurity feelings related to early childhood when fears could not be escaped physically because one had no power over one's legs or general movements. The dream is accordingly interpreted as a desire for a certain experience (one is perhaps being 'chased' by one's emotions) being unsatisfied by reason of the fear of failure or the inability to face the required experience. The traditional oracles tend to ignore this convincing interpretation and present a dream of paralysis as portending such things as arguments within the family circle, and general dishonour. A dream in which one is wanting to run away but cannot is interpreted by the commonplace Zolar's Book of Dreams as meaning that the dreamer will have a big sickness, and yet a similar dream of being unable to run away in the face of some fear means that the dreamer will go into exile.

For a man to dream that he is being buried **29** signifies that he shall have as much wealth as he has ground laid over him.

Illustrating the typical dream of being rooted to the spot, or of being paralysed, which is so very often accompanied by monsters menacing in the background (see page 55). Such a dream is often a throwback to early childhood experiences before adequate physical mobility was possible, and sometimes it is even related to pre-natal experiences of restriction in the womb or in the vaginal passage at birth. The dream may be interpreted in terms of a need-to 'grow up'–to develop a sense of responsibility–for the need to develop physically is equated with the need to develop emotionally. Thus a dream of being trapped is related to impotence and inadequacy feelings. In this dream the woman cannot move because she is almost buried in stones and earth, and the very barrenness of the landscape suggests that she feels restricted by the environment in which she lives. The menacing hand may be interpreted as symbolic of the hostility of those who resent her presence in this environment where she is a stranger. It is to be noted that she is not facing the hostility, yet she is still deeply afraid, suggesting that she will not recognise openly the factors which are giving rise to her fears.

NIGHTMARES

30 The dream symbolism of rising and falling is fairly
obvious, and the ancient meaning which has
persisted into modern times, is revealed in the
Talmud:

> Anyone who climbs on to a roof will obtain
> dignities, whilst anyone who climbs down will
> be dishonoured.
> To dream of a fall from a high place, or form a
> high tree denotes many troubles will follow.

The reverse dream of moving upwards, in whatever
way, has a favourable significance.

> To dream you are flying is a good dream, shows
> great success in life, and happiness in love.

Dreams of falling tend to be remembered more than
dreams of climbing—indeed, there is a certain kind
of dream which is fairly commonly experience of
being awakened abruptly almost as soon as one has
gone to sleep by this dream of falling. This kind of
dream has been related to a fall in blood pressure as
we go to sleep, to physical posture in which sleep
commences, and to the atavistic remnants of the fear
of falling when we lived and slept in trees. The
traditional oracles do not appear to connect any of
these interpretations with their symbols:

> Being injured in a fall means that you will
> endure hardships and loose friends. A dream of
> falling from a bridge means madness A dream of
> falling into the sea means a woman's love will
> bring dishonour.

On the other hand, the dream of flying finds a great
similarity between the traditional oracles and

modern psychological interpretations. All the ancient oracles interpret this kind of dream favourably-especially if one dreams that one is flying without wings, for this signifies liberation, riches and a rise in position accompanied with an increase in power. A long flight means that one will make a long and profitable journey.

> To dream you are flying is a good dream, for it showeth great success in life, and happiness in love.

31 Even the modernised oracles of the traditional kind have preserved the favourable flavour of these dreams when introducing aeroplanes and flying saucers. We learn, for instance, that a flight in an aeroplane is a sign of a profitable speculation ahead, whilst a dream of actually owning a plane means 'success in all undertakings'.

It is not surprising that modern psychologists suggest that a dream wherein one has the power to fly implies an expression of a power urge. Sometimes the dream is interpreted as a wish to escape, and sometimes as a wish to surmount natural limitations. Certain psychologists have explained such dreams as ancient memory traces of the times when our ancestors floated on the sea, and such interpretations are no less far—fetched than those of the psychical experimenters who say that 'flying' dreams are actually memories of the astral body freed of the material body, which is, according to them, the normal condition of sleep.

The witchhunters of a few centuries ago found that the simplest way to prove guilt of flying was to equate the delusion with the act, so that if a woman actually dreamed that she had flown to a sabbat, she was just as guilty as if she really had mounted her broom stick and flown. In fact, the popular image of a broom stick as the vehicle of flight for witches is not so accurate, for a shovel, a distaff, a pitchfork or a cleft stick were equally efficacious. Animals, such as goats, dogs and oxen were also used for flying. The ringing of church bells was a sufficient power to crash all such 'broom sticks', and it is recorded that in the seventeenth century all the churches in Trèves were ordered to ring their bells throughout the nights of May in order to protect the city from witches flying over.

An ancient spell for flying by use of magic is interesting:

This ritual must be undertaken only once a year, **32** on the twenty fifth of June, when the Sun is in Cancer. You take a stag's skin and make two garters from it, and write in each of them the above hieroglyphics. This writing must be done with the blood of a hare which was killed on the same day. On this day also, but before the sun is risen, you must gather an amount of green mugwort, and cut a short rod from a holm-oak. Both garters are filled with the mugwort, and one eye of a barbel fish is then placed in each. When it is desired to fly, the wizard rises before the sun and washes his garters in a running stream, and then puts them on above the knee. He then points the oak rod in the direction in which he wants to fly, writes the name of the place in which he wants to land on the ground. The garters will fly at once, carrying the wizard. To stop, he must wave the wand in the air and say AMECH.

33 Related to the flying dreams are the hanging dreams, which are certainly nightmarish in quality:

To see people hanged, or to feel hung yourself,
Is the manifest proof of the increase of pelf;
And however awkward we own the sensation,
You scarcely dare doubt of a just elevation.

To dream of falling into a pit shows that some **34** very heavy misfortune is about to attend you, and that your sweatheart is false and prefers another; to a sailor the dream bodes some sad disaster at the next port he arrives at.

To climb a high ladder, prognosticates sure, **35**
Of a high elevation and wealth to the poor.
To the single a marriage, with virtue and worth,
Tough equivocal to folks of high birth.
To fall down a ladder then entails a curse.
Thro' sleeping or waking naught well can be worse.

A grave in a dream fatal sickness will prove; **36**
And a barrier obtrudes to the object you love.

The well-known and often beautiful flying dream is very often an expression of an inferiority feeling. In flight one is free and omnipotent—removed from the world with all its snares and restrictions which so weigh down the personality. The particular dream illustrated, which is one of a city 'gent' flying over the city itself may be related to such interpretations in terms of a wish to rise above the monolithic city (represented by the skyscraper blocks) out of the conditions where the individual is lost as a minor particle in a huge whole. This is an expression of a real inner need to escape to a place of quiet, where one may become aware of onself as a differentiated being with a life and purpose of ones own, where one is not simply participating as a cell unit of a monster body. From a point of view of Freudian dream interpretation, however, such a dream may be seen in terms of latent homosexuality, for the emotional demands of such a kind separate the dreamer from the common herd, and the skyscraper blocks may be seen as so many phallic symbols reaching out towards him suggesting 'places of security'.

In the dream of a man being caught up in a series of machines we see an expression of a panic at the idea of being destroyed by the technocratic, Kafkaesque world around us. Schizophrenics often attempt to give organic things (such as their own bodies) a mechanical forms in expression of the wish to introduce an element of control over themselves or their environment. Organic things in dreams very often seem to be mechanical because in this form they may be manipulated and controlled by the dreamer. Often the reverse of such a dream (such as the one illustrated) is where the mechanical elements take on a life and form of their own and become organic when, for instance, a car turns into a living thing, and refuses to be driven, indicating a state of affairs in which their is no conscious control. We see, therefore, that the frightening dream of a loss in control is closely related to the fear of a loss of identity. One part of our mind genuinely believes that we control ourselves and our lives, whilst another part believes quite the opposite. The two minds are at loggerheads in this kind of nightmare.

62

NATURE

The dream illustrated is of the 'horses, carriage and driver' variety which is discussed on page 65. The specific interpretation must be related to the case of the dreamer herself, and in general terms we can see a strong sexual element as the roots of the dream The emotions, symbolised by the horses, are out of control, and the carriage, usually identified with the body of the dreamer, is full of men who are much larger than they should be in terms of the scale, suggesting that the dreaming woman is prepossesed with sex, and feels trapped by her own emotional needs. Her anxiety is triggering off an almost nightmarish dream which expresses her lack of emotional control in a very vivid imagery.

NATURE
and dreams

37 IN all the ancient oracles the Earth in a dream is interpreted as a symbol of the female, so that planting a seed in the earth, or working a field with a plough, is related either to fecundity or sex. Artemidorus, like Freud after him, regarded the plough and the furrow as a symbol of the male member and the vagina. It is scarcely surprising, therefore, that the traditional oracles tend to think of a field of grass or a patch of earth as relating to the female, so that they may interpret a dream of a green field as meaning that relationships at home will be good, and a dream of working in the fields as meaning that a child will shortly be born into the family.

Owning land in a dream means that you will have a good wife.

A dream of a farmer working the earth means that big profits will come to you.

A dream of pleasant pastures means that you will have good children.

To see or to saunter among the green fields,
Foretells that dame Fortune propitiously yields;
To lovers and tradesmen, success and great wealth;
To farmers a plenitude, riches and health.

Dreams of water have always received much **38** attention from interpreters, and although there is much disagreement as to the individual significance of such dreams it is generally admitted that water is related to birth, the mother and children. Thus we see that Artemidorus interprets a man's dream of a stream running along a meadow to mean that he will soon marry a young woman and have children, and another dream of a spring running through his house is interpreted as meaning that his wife will have a bad name. On this level, Artemidorus has the same attitude to water as Freud, who tended to see it as relating to the uterine waters, so that a dream of going down to the sea is, within his framework of interpretation, an incest wish to return to the mother's womb. Such a dream is therefore escapist—just as waking thoughts of taking a ship 'to get away from it all' are escapist. The connexion between Artemidorus and Freud is, of course, the *anima*, the woman in which every man may escape himself, and the clues to interpretation is the condition of the water itself. If the water is clear and in its right place (not running through a house, for example!) then the man will surely find his *anima*, and all will be well. If the water is tainted or otherwise unusual, the the man will not find what he needs. The link between the sea and the mother is particularly insistent in mythology where we find many gods being born from the sea —Aphrodite is perhaps the most famous example —the idea being that they were born 'of nature yet without human intervention'. The traditional oracles retain this connexion between water and birth; for example, being offered a glass of water means the birth of a child, whilst drinking from a glass of water means the drinker will be married shortly. (One wonders how to interpret a dream of a young woman in which she is offered a glass of water, takes it and drinks!) The following traditional oracles, culled from Zolar, will prove the point:

To dream of carrying water into a bedroom   39

means that one will be visited by a man with loose morals. Drawing water from a fountain means that a beautiful wife will bring a fortune. Breaking a glass filled with water means the death of a mother, though health for her children. A girl dreaming of a stormy sea will soon be anguished by a double-cross.

A dream of a high tide at sea certainly means fortune in business, whilst a low tide means adversity.

Other oracles support the general idea that water is a good dream image:

Waterfalls mean adverse troubles and strife,
But where flowing smoothly so flows your life;
When water looks thick, difficulties are near,
But most happy you, when 'tis seen to look clear.
Swimming in water, good fortune promotes,
But immersed beneath, tribulation denotes.
The dream of being in a shower of rain, be it gentle and soft, denotes great success in your affairs. It is very favourable to lovers, and it denotes constancy, affection and sweet temper.

Few people know the origin of the St. Swithun legend which maintains that if it rains on the fifteenth of July, it will rain for forty days. It is said that St. Swithun, who died in 862 AD, asked to be buried in an ordinary graveyard, so that the rain could fall upon him, and he could have ordinary men passing over his head. Although his wish was carried out, some few years afterwards the monks of Winchester decided that so great a saint should have a better tomb, and they accordingly tried to move his remains.   This work began on July

15th, but it was not finished because of the torrential downpour which continued unabated for forty days. His body was not moved for over a century after his death. The legend still persists, in spite of every proof that should dispel it.

A fire in a dream is one of the richest of all symbols, **40** though it is capable of many possible interpretations, depending on the circumstances of the dream itself. One modern survey of the interpretation of dreams has shown five different kinds of meanings which may be attributed to a dream of a fire, depending on the nature of the fire itself, and these include love (also sexual love), riches, the king, head of state (in other words the supreme principle and so on) and war, the destructive powers. A small fire, such as a hearth fire, has a pleasant significance, whilst a large fire, especially a conflagration, presages evil. The interpretation is clearly based on the dual nature of fire itself, for fire may warm and keep alive (and is often linked in this state with the emotions) and yet it may also destroy and consume (the emotions out of control). There is no contradiction between Artemidorus' interpretation of a small hearth fire meaning good luck ahead, and the ancient Egyptian oracle which says that a large fire presages the death of the dreamer's son or brother.

A dream of a fire without smoke means that shortly a love affair will be ended, and this shows the common identification of a dream fire with love —the hearth fire, in particular, is linked with the idea of a female (the associations of the hearth, the kitchen fire, the frying pan and the chimney, with its uterine significance) with whom the dreamer is very possibly in love. This association has persisted into all modern oracles, though several tend to shy away from the obvious sexual implications of such dreams as 'poking a fire', and so on.

A dream of sitting alone by a fireside means that you are happy in love, and sitting at the fireside with your fiance means that you will soon get married—though, sitting with others by the fire means that you are being deceived by friends.

41 Freud identifies the sun in a dream with the father of the dreamer, but in doing this he was merely following in the ancient tradition of dream interpretation which has always identified the sun with the king (a father image) and with power or authority.

The traditional oracles are not so precise as Freud, and there is a tendency to link the condition of the sun in the dream with the future condition of the dreamer himself: thus, a dark sun or a setting sun implies that the fortunes of the dreamer will be on the decline, whilst a sunrise implies coming success, and a glimpse of the 'silver lining' or the sun peeping through the clouds is a sign that one's present troubles will shortly disappear. If a woman dreams of a beautiful sunset, a child is on the way —and in fact the only unpleasant interpretation of a bright sun is the one in which one dreams of a sun shining over a house, for this means that there will be a fire in that house. To see blood on the sun, or the colour of blood on the sun means an accident will befall you soon.

42 The Moon is regarded by almost all oracles as either a symbol of the mother of the dreamer or of a woman, and it is associated with good luck, so that

LA·LUNE

a dream of the full moon, for example, means coming joy, and if the moon is unclouded, it means success in love. Artemidorus says that for a man to dream of seeing himself in the moon means that he will have a son, whilst for a woman to see herself mirrored in the moon means that she will have a daughter. Thus it is not surprising that the oneiromancer Gegafar should interpret a man's dream of 'embrasing the moon' as meaning a marriage to the most beautiful woman in the country, and a subsequent dream of carrying the moon in his hands as a sign that the marriage would result in the birth of a most beautiful son.

Daniel is the only dream interpreter who is not in accord with the usual identification with women: in his interpretations a small moon means that a prince will be killed, a falling moon is a sign of coming difficulties, whilst a dream of many moons indicates violence to the dreamer.

> Many draw varied imports from this lamp of the night,
> To some it bodes sorrow, to ethers delight;
> But always more joyous when seen shining bright.

A few fixed selections from the traditional oracles will round off this section:

43   To dream of an eclipse of the sun means that you will lose some male friend; of an eclipse of the moon that you will lose some female friend.

To dream of an earthquake means that some great change is at hand in your life.

44   To dream you are in a hailstorm presages great sorrow in life by the divulging important secrets.

When sliding on ice so gaily along,   **45**
In whistling a tune or in chanting a song,
Your hopes all expectant may meet a frustration,
For all those who slide must hazard prostration.

In general animals in dreams represent the   **46**
undirected passions and instincts in man. Jung goes
so far as to suggest that in a dream man actually
puts in a symbolic human or animal form the things·
which he fears. This is probably the reason why it
is possible to dream that animals can speak a human
language, and why such a dream always suggests a
state of unhappiness to come. To dream of fighting
wild animals indicates an illness is on the way, but
to dream of domesticated animals indicates a certain
peace and tranquility will follow. The significance
of each animal, where it is recognisable in a dream,
varies considerably however, and it is therefore wise
to look into the meaning of each for exact interpretation. For fierce or frightening animals which
cannot be recognised, see *Nightmares*. From the
very earliest times oracles have tended to interpret
the appearance of the horse in a dream as the
embodiment of the passion and sometimes with the
woman. Thus, to dream of a horse is to dream of the
life force in one way or another, and it is hardly
surprising that the horse stands as the double symbol
of the woman and death, for a moving horse
repesents the passions moving in time towards the
one inevitable end. The victorian dream oracles,
although they tended to base their interpretations on
the ancient traditions, were in the strange position
of witnessing the decline in importance of the horse
in social life, and consequently many of the interpretations of this time have been passed over to other

forms of transport, with a considerable weakening of the interpretation accorded to the 'dream horse'. A random selection from such a source suggests that a dream of a horse running away betokens misfortune (emotions out of control), a dream of a female horse means an early marriage to a beautiful woman, a castrated horse means happiness and a dead horse that you will have a good yearly earning. Something of the old flavour remains, however, in the interpretation of a dream in which friends of the dreamer are riding a horse, for it means that these friends will commit adultery with the dreamer's wife!

A horse with four white feet is supposed to be lucky. One custom in several parts of England on seeing a white horse is to spit and wish, and to keep one's fingers crossed until one sees a dog.
It is still believed in the North of England that it is possible to cure whooping-cough by holding a child near to a horse's mouth so that it may breath on the face.

47 Almost all oracles agree that a monkey in a dream represents a charlatan, though it may well represent the charlatan tendencies of the dreamer himself. Sometimes it is a symbol of an enemy. Thus, to dream of chattering monkeys means that you will be flattered by a deceitful friend. If the dream monkey is in a cage you will encounter difficulties in love, but if it is climbing a tree your enemies will seek your downfall.

48 Artemidorus identifies a cat in a dream with adultery on the grounds that cats attack and devour birds, and birds are symbols of women! Others identify cats with thieves, and the modern interpretation tends to be that a cat is a symbol for a woman closely connected with the dreamer. Thus cats in dreams do not have a very good reputation, and their presence is connected with widely separated events such as loss of property, adultery and divorce. As one dream book puts it:

Of these emblems of trouble no one is a stranger,
They amplify poverty, sickness and danger.

Whilst Artemidorus identifies domesticated dogs in **49** dreams with women and servants, other interpreters think the dog of any kind represents the dreamer's enemies. In particular, the black dog is associated with the devil and his attendant evils, and one is warned to beware of treachery after such a dream. The interpretation of the meaning to be perceived in the different breeds of dogs varies a good deal. A dream of a greyhound, for example, means that you will be seduced, whilst a dream of a bulldog means that you will quarrel with a girl friend. A yelping dog implies danger ahead, and a dream of a male dog playing with a bitch means that lovers are being unfaithful to each other.

Artemidorus mentions that the appearance of a dog in a dream may presage a fever, since the star Sirius, which is called the *dog-star*, rules over fevers.

To see dogs in a dream, if they fondle 'tis joy;
But if they should bite you, some foes will annoy.
If you dream that a bullock pursues you, beware of some powerful enemy, particularly if you are female. If a cow pursues you, the enemy is a female.

50 According to the Egyptian book of dreams, if you should see yourself eating the flesh of an ass or donkey, it means that you will shortly gain financially. If you dream that you are riding a donkey this means that you will fall into social disgrace, though being pulled by a donkey indicates a coming love affair which will turn out well unless the dream donkey should kick you. The donkey in the dream is the passive body—'brother ass' as Saint Francis called it—which is not doing what it should be doing. That is why a dream of a donkey suggests someone who has a duty to perform: whether he will or will not perform the duty must be interpreted from what the donkey is doing. A donkey being loaded, for example, indicates that business will go well in the future. According to the Persian dream oracles, for a pregnant woman to dream of an ass is not good, for it means that she will loose the child. For a man to dream that his donkey is dead means that he himself will die quite soon.

To dream that you ride a donkey is a sign that you will shortly have an opportunity of being happily married.

51 To dream of a fox is not good, for this crafty animal is the forerunner of much difficulty; if you are in love, your sweetheart will turn out to be of a sour, disagreable and illnatured disposition.

52 Like most other animals in dreams, the hare stands for the human passions and desires, and it is therefore not surprising that the majority of dream oracles have linked this animal with a woman and in particular with a prostitute. A dream of chasing a hare has been interpreted both as a sign of a forthcoming marriage and as a wish to seek the services of a harlot. The reader must draw his own conclusions! Other oracles suggest that a dream of a hare is simply a dream of one's enemies. In the north of England it is regarded as unlucky to meet a hare on the same path 'see below' and to see a hare running through a village main street is a sure indication of a coming fire, and such beliefs have probably coloured the majority of dream interpretations.

In Cornwall it is believed that girls who die of forsaken love turn into white hares and pursue their betrayers. The general feeling that it is unlucky to meet a hare, and the old custom of crossing onself on seeing a hare (a custom by no means dead at present) is due to the ancient popular belief that witches could turn themselves into hares, and thus when one saw a hare one might in fact be seeing a witch in disguise! In certain parts of England children are told that it is the hare which lays Easter Eggs—this again has an ancient origin, for in pre-Christian times the hare was regarded as sacred, and its flesh was forbidden to ordinary men. Some people believe that a hare's right foor carried in the pocket keeps away rheumatism.

To dream of elephants is a sign of coming **53** property, and that some friends will greatly assist you, and that you will marry above your station.

Rats in dreams signify enemies, and that you are **54** exposed to many dangers from pretended friends.

A spell from the seventeenth century sets the recipe for preparing a stone to warn people of ills:

Take a great toad and kill it, and then put it into a horse dung hill until the ants have consumed his flesh. In the head you will find a thing like a stone, and this should be set in gold and worn about the body, for it does give warning of mischief or ill for the wearer by changing colours.

55 Incidentally, toads in dreams presage difficulties—a dream of catching a toad means self inflicted injuries are on the way. A frog, on the other hand, is a good thing—hearing frogs croaking means pleasure ahead, and eating frogs means wealth in the offing. There is the same interpretation as for toads, however, should you try to catch your frog! The problem appears that one should try to kill the frog in the dream without actually catching it first:

> Toad creatures are noxious, typifying e'en the Devil,
> But kill them, you'll conquer your foes and all evil!

56 A goat in a dream is 'a good thing', for even killing a goat brings happiness, whilst a baby goat means success in gambling and a plain ordinary goat with no frills attached means that you will be rich. One dream book records that only poor people who dream of goats will be rich, for those already rich at the time of the dream will meet with dishonour.

57 There are several interpretations given to the appearance of snakes in dreams. On the one hand, because it is a belief that snakes live in holes in the ground, the snake is held by the ancient Egyptian oracles, to be a guardian of hidden treasures, and consequently the appearance of a snake in a dream implies that riches will follow. It is also believed that should the snake bite the dreamer then a lawsuit is predicted, and should the dreamer kill the snake, then certain quarrels will soon be over. On the other hand, Artemidorus teaches that a snake in a dream presages a long illness, and in Talmudic literature there are even more contradictory teachings. A snake in a zoo means that friends are not grateful, whilst a coiled snake means that the dreamer will escape a danger. Killing a snake means that the dreamer will be victorious over enemies —and indeed it is not uncommon (or unreasonable) for oracles to treat a snake in a dream as an image of the dreamer's enemy. In modern dream interpretations the tendency is to regard the snake as as sexual symbol, and as such it may be interpreted only within the framework of the dreamer's unique psychological background—this probably accounts for the confusion of different meanings attributed to the snake in dreams: one man's enemy may be another man's fecundity symbol! Outside the realm of dreams, the snake is regarded as an omen all over the world. In Britian one who sees a live adder near the front door of a house knows that someone living in the house will die. It is generally believed in country districts that snakes cannot die before sunset, even if they are very badly hurt. It is also believed that snakes hate ashtrees, and it is possible to kill a snake (even before sunset) by striking it with a branch of ash. For this reason a man carrying an ash branch or wearing a sprig of ash twigs is considered to be quite immune to snakes even in an infested area. Good luck and protection from fire

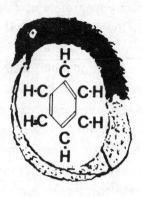

can be assured to those who hang a dried adder's
skin on the roof of their house!

A curious dream of a snake has gone down in the
history of dream interpretation. The German
chemist Kekule had been trying for several years to
find a way of graphically presenting the structure
of benzene. In a dream be saw "structures of
different forms and in a long chain ... everything
was moving in a snake-like and twisting manner.
Suddenly, what was this? One of the snakes had hold
of its own tail and the whole structure was mockingly
twisting in front of my eyes!" In the dream he had
seen the Ouroboros serpent biting it's own tail, and
this had enabled him to draw up the molecular
structure of benzene.

58   A worm is envy, in friendship's disguise,
To what in our estimate mostly we prize.

In dreams reptiles in general indicate hidden
enemies, and thus if you dream of killing a reptile

you are dealing successfully with some treacherous people. If in a dream you meet anyone holding or owning a reptile you must be careful of this person —especially if you recognize him. If you should dream of dying from the bite of a reptile, you should be especially wary of business dealings with people whom you do not know well. A dream of relatives or friends dying of reptile bites means that people are talking about you in evil terms.

In Ireland it is believed that if a person licks a lizard all over, his tongue will ever afterwards have healing properties, and he will be able to cure sores by licking the affected parts.

It is unlucky if a lizard crosses the path of a wedding party on the way to the church.

Take the liver of a chameleon and burn it on the top of a house, when great storms of thunder and lightenings will manifest.

Although a dream of ants generally promises well **59** for the future, there are two exceptions to the rule. Artemidorus maintains that since ants belong to the earth and are both black and cold they resemble death itself, and consequently a dream of ants crawling over one's body or crawling into one's ears, means that the dreamer will die shortly. Similarly, to dream of ants in a house means that someone from that particular house will be ill very soon. To see ants under almost any other circumstances means well, since ants are associated with industry, and thus an ant dream predicts an increase in business and wealth. The modern dream interpreter Stekel suggests that ants represent people from the same household as the dreamer. In Cornwall ants are thought to be fairies in the last stage of existence on Earth. It was believed that if a piece of tin was placed in an ant's nest during the time of the new moon, this would turn to silver.

60 A seventeenth century cure for swellings:

> Take off the head of a small ant, and bruise the body between your fingers and anoint with it any impostumated tumour, and it will presently sink down.

61 A dream of flies and other vermin denotes enemies of all sorts, but to dream of killing them is a good omen.

62 A dream of caterpillars means that you will experience great vexation, mischief, resentment and malice.

63 To dream of bees or the buzzing of bees indicates trouble is coming, and most oracles interpret being stung by a bee as meaning a physical hurt – though:

> Whenever they sting you your fame will be tarnished,
> Howe'er by your riches or good fortune varnished!

Rich people who dream of bees will have upsets in business—tough poor people will find an increase in their earnings. The place in which you see the bees indicates the situation or direction in which the trouble will be found: if they swarm into your own house, then the trouble will come from one of your enemies. If the bees are making honey rather than swarming or stinging, then things will not be so bad, for if they are making honey on your own land, your business venture will be successful—should you dream that you kill the bee, then your undertakings will fail through your own fault.

A dream of many bats indicates a death within **64** the family circle. To dream of one grey bat means that you will have an easy life in the future, but a black bat means a quarrel and a white bat means that a sick acquaintance will recover.

From a Victorian spellbook:

> Bats. These little evening visitors are considered lucky in love affairs. If one flies across your path when you are walking with your lover, the circumstances indicate the illness either of yourself or your sweetheart. If they fly against the windows of the room in which you are in company with your lover, it signifies the opposition of your sweethearts parents to your keeping company together, but if you see one dead, it means that your lover will pay his addresses without opposition or rivalry interfering.

Stekel suggests that all flying things are symbols of death.

In view of the scarcity of crocodiles in England it **65** is hardly worth while recording the Egyptian belief that a dream of eating fish means that you will be swallowed by such a creature, yet the belief has to a certain extent persisted in the sense that such a dream implies big worries ahead—unless the fish be boiled, in which case one has joy to look forward to.

Most oracles identify the fish with one's hopes and so to catch a lot of fish brings much good, whilst to lose a fish, or to find a fish dead is a bad augury. Birckmayer suggests that fish in dreams symbolize past events 'because fishes are silent', yet even he links the fish with hopes and dreams of advancement. The modern school tends to regard fish as symbols for either the child of the dreamer or for the dreamer himself. The phallic connexion needs no further comment.

In certain places fish have been held to be sacred, which partly accounts for the linking of Christ with fish, as the 'Fisher of Men', and occasionally fish in ponds or well were regarded as being the 'spirits' of the water. These fish were sacrosanct, and it was forbidden to harm them in any way. The result is that even today there are ponds and wells where there are so many fish (since they have never been harmed, but more often than not have been well fed) that they can scarcely move and their bodies are badly bruised by their continual knocking together in the water.

66 A victorian dream oracle says of a fishing dream:

> To many proves often the token of care,
> And to maidens in love I would counsel 'beware'.
> If fish shall be caught 'tis to lovers all well;
> But slipp'd thro' your hand, disappointments there dwell.
> But all fish in general predict vacillation,
> With friends some dissension and prevarication.

67 Most oracles agree that birds in dreams augur well —the bird is either a harbinger of peace or it represents peace-loving men and women. The arab interpreters insist that unrecognised birds in dreams are actually angels. Thus, to see a bird in a dream presages success in ones undertakings, and to capture a bird means gains ahead—even marriage, according to at least one oracle. However, a vision of sea birds means disappointments in business. To dream of birds coming out of the egg implies good news will shortly be heard, and to see eggs in a nest means that a large payment of money will shortly be made to you.

Birds in dreams are often symbols of women, and **68** one modern dream book records an interpretation of the famous Ibn Sirin as an example of almost Freudian insight. A man came to Ibn Sirin and recounted his dream in which three times he tried to cut the throat of a bird, and yet only at the fourth attempt was he successful. Sirin said that the bird was actually a woman whom the dreamer must have tried to seduce three times so far, and at the next attempt he would be successful. Obviously Sirin saw in the knife a symbol of the penis, and in the bird the transference of a 'low desire' of sex into a higher sphere (the image of a bird which flies high)—which is fairly typical dream inversion. The act of aggression (cutting the bird's throat) was obviously a sexual act which was being resisted by the victim. Sometimes birds are regarded as bringing news of

death—a bird tapping at the window pane or flying
down the chimney (literally, entering the body—see
Body) is such an omen. The impending death of
the Bishop of Salisbury is supposed to be predicted
by the appearance of two large white birds which sail
through the air without moving their wings, and
this omen has been recorded as late as 1911. A similar
belief is held in Sussex concerning the death of the
Bishop of Chichester—the omen being the appearance
of a heron perching on the Cathedral building.

69   To hear warblers sing, is a token of health;
To catch them, of risng to some sudden wealth;
Of finding a nest without young, tells dismay,
Disappointment of prospect and hope ev'ry way;
In a word, singing birds, whereso'er you may see,
Indicate you prosperity, honour and glee!

To dream of an owl is a bad omen, however, for it
fortells sickness, poverty and imprisonment. It also
forewarns you that some male friend will turn out
perfidious, and endeavour to do you a great injury,
in which without the utmost caution on your part,
he will succeed.

An ancient magical spell records that if you take
the heart and right foot of shrike owl and place
them over a man whilst he is sleeping he will tell
you whatsoever you ask of him!

70   Eggs are symbols both of birth and money. Thus,

having fresh eggs betokens that you will receive money presently, and having broken eggs means loss of money.

In some parts of England it is the custom to break egg shells after having scooped out the egg meat. This custom originated from the belief that witches used egg shells as boats to cross the sea.

If you dream you hear the cuckoo, your sweetheart **71** will prove a coquette.

To dream you see or hear a blackbird a female will have two husbands, and a male two wives.

To dream you see pigeons flying, imports hasty news of a very pleasant nature, and success in all your undertakings.

Seeing a peacock in your dreams denotes great success in trade: to a man, a beautiful wife, to a maid, a good rich husband; to a widow, that she will be courted by one who will tell her many fine tales without being sincere; it also denotes great prosperity by sea, and a handsome wife in a distant part.

A dream of geese also denotes success and riches in life. In love they augur fidelity to your sweetheart and a speedy marriage.

The nightingale in particular is a sure forerunner of joyful news, and of great success in business, of plentiful crops, and a sweet tempered lover.

THINGS

Dreams of just missing the bus or train may obviously be interpreted in relation to fears of inadequacy concerning ones position in society and in the universe—one is not able to do what one wants to do—the dreamer can see what he wants, but he cannot quite get it. The nature of the frustration may well be determined by the other factors in the dream; if for example the dreamer misses the bus on the way to work in the morning, then the frustration may be involved with work, with the dreamers ambitions or with some personality in his profession. On the other hand, a dream of missing the bus on the way home in the evening suggests that the frustrating element may be found in the home or in the way one spends ones leisure hours. By extension, being unable to make the car start in order to drive to work, or the train breaking down on the way home, may be interpreted in similar terms. This type of dream is familiar to almost everyone, and its frequent recurrence suggests that something practical should be done to alleviate the frustration which the dream pinpoints.

THINGS
in dreams

To dream of possessing money implies that you will have financial gains, though even the reverse dream of losing money, is taken to mean that success is on the way. As one victorian oracles puts it:

> If gold, it is lucky; but should it be copper,
> It claps on your fortune a sad weighty stopper.

A dream of finding money in the street means that there is danger of business losses, and although the usual interpretation of finding money in the form of treasure is usually interpreted as a portent of impending danger there is at least one recorded dream which proves the contrary. A fifteenth century tinker from Swaffham, one John Chapman, dreamed that if he went to London and stood on London Bridge a stranger would give him some information which would lead him to a great fortune. He did as the dream advised, and he did indeed meet a man who told him that he too had had a dream—this to the effect that a pedlar from Swaffham had a pot of money buried on his land. Chapman returned home and, sure enough, he discovered the money. He helped to build a church in Suffolk with part of the money, and a statue to his memory still stands in the church.

> A dream of diamonds is an excellent dream, for it shows that some unexpected success will raise you above your present position in life.

Iron or steel nails in dreams invariably indicate trouble in one form or another. For example, to dream of hammering nails indicates that a divorce is on the way. Only when one dreams of selling nails is one likely to expect success, for copper nails mean sorrow, steel nails illness, and large nails indicate heavy losses.

Radford records a ritual in Suffolk for curing diseases and worms in children. Nine nails, drawn from nine different horseshoes, were boiled in urine. The two people who were working this spell had to communicate by signs as complete silence was required for it to work. The ritual was begun at midnight, and the urine was boiled until it was strong enough to set three, five or seven nails in motion at once. When the patient cried out, it was a sign that the hold of the illness had been broken.

74 Bells ringing betoken good news to all folks,
Yet in wedlock prognosticate unpleasant jokes.

75 To dream of wearing chains in a jail means that business will be bad for a short time, but to dream of chains which are not attached to your body means that you will escape from some difficulty. To break a chain in your dreams means that you will have worrying problems for a short while. Actually, dream oracles tend to be very contradictory about chains, for whilst the Egyptian oracle maintains that chains presage good events ('for it means that a man will not leave his family'), Artemidorus regards them purely and simply as symbols of obstacles which bode no good.

In a dream an unopened letter means an un- **76** revealed secret, whilst an open letter means news which is generally known. Writing a letter means that you will be imparting some information to the person to whom you are writing in the dream. A letter is a means of communicating with someone whom it is either difficult or undesirable to see in person, and the dream must be interpreted accordingly. Receiving letters is interpreted by one oracle thus:

> The arrival we here apprehend of some news,
> The remittance of money or gifts that amuse;
> But if the contents you should fail to connect,
> Disappointments you'll meet where you least will expect.

There is an old spell with a love letter which is supposed to enable a young lady to dream of her beloved's intent. On receiving such a letter she must lay it wide open, and fold it into nine folds. She should then pin it next to her heart until bed time. The folded letter should then be placed in her left-hand glove, which is put under her pillow. If she dreams of gold or costly gems her lover is true and does indeed mean what he says. If however she dreams of white linen she will lose him by death, and if she dreams of flowers he is certainly false. If she should dream of the lover himself he is false and means none of his endearing terms, wishing only to draw the young lady into a trap!

77 To dream of an anchor implies some success,
But warns you of person's you're prone to caress.
So beware well of him, who of friendship pretends,
He will clearly deceive you to gain his own ends.

78 To dream of a candle burning brightly means that you will receive a letter from a dear friend. To dream of putting out lighted candles means a quarrel with a friend, whilst to light a candle means that you will meet a new friend, and to dream of

being burned by a candle means that you will have a serious accident. If a sick person dreams he sees a clear lighted candle burning upon a table, it denotes recovery and health—he that dreams this and is unmarried, will soon be married. A lighted torch or lantern denotes the same.

A light that burns both bright and clear,
Denotes some pleasant letter near.
But if dull the candle grows,
It certain disappointment shows.

Candles have many interesting superstitions attached to them. If a flame of a candle burns blue it is said that there is a spirit in the house, or not far away. A lighted candle is supposed to be a protection against evil spells. The custom in Ireland of burning twelve candles around a dead body prior to burial is founded on this belief, for they are intended to keep off evil spirits who are, by their very nature, unable to cross a burning ring of fire, and thus cannot carry of the dead man's soul. Folklore holds that it is unlucky to burn three candles in one room at any one time. Wax candles are used in Churches (it is said) because there is a tradition that bees come from paradise.

79 There are also numerous oracles and spells built around candles. For example, it is believed that when a candle shoots off sparks, then a letter will shortly be received by the one nearest to where the sparks land. If a candle should gutter out when there is no wind at hand, then this indicates a death in the family. Women who want to divine the state of their lover's affections may use a candle to establish the truth. A pin must be pushed through a candle half way down, in such a way that it actually pierces the wick. Whilst she is doing this she must repeat the following rhyme:

> It is not this candle along I stick,
> But . . .'s heart I mean to prick;
> Whether he be asleep or awake.
> I'll have him come to me and speak.

She must then watch the candle as it burns away, and if the pin remains in the wick after the flame has made its way below the place in which it was inserted she may go to rest with an easy mind. If the pin drops out, however, it is a sign that he is faithless and not worth thinking about any more.

80 If you dream you are in bed, it implies that you

will be married before the end of the month!

To dream the clock strikes, and you count but **81** that instant it stands still, forebodes death to some old friend, but if the hand moves again, the party will recover.

If you dream that you loose your hat or shoes, it **82** denotes that you will quickly be married.

A ring is usually a symbol of the marital state, and **83** to dream of receiving a ring indicates a coming marriage or affair. To dream of losing a ring indicates the loss of a dear friend (not a loss by death however) — similarly, a dream of a broken ring indicates a broken relationship. The ringstone itself affects the interpretation of a dream — expensive stones presage good, whilst cheap or broken stones indicate loss or difficulties. Artemidorus tells a story of a man who dreamed that he threw away his signet ring, and when he recovered it the stone was broken into fifty five pieces — needless to say, exactly fifty five days later he lost his entire fortune.

There is an old ritual to determine how many years must elapse before you marry:

Pull a hair from your head, fasten a ring to it, and dangle it in a jug. The ring vibrates or swings, and so often as it touches the side of the jug, so many years it will be before you will marry.

A dream of flowers indicates great prosperity ahead, **84** though the interpretation does vary, depending on the kind of flower in the dream. A narcissus, for instance, is a troublesome thing to see, according to Artemidorus — especially for sailors or for those about to make voyages at sea. Again, though white violets indicate coming troubles, and blue violets mean death, a dream of plucking violets indicates that marriage will go well in the future. Although it is generally advantageous to dream of spring roses, a dream of rose trees is only favourable to those who actually plant them or grow them, as to others they presage difficulties and long journeys. Freud is not alone in seeing a sexual significance in flowers—for the heads of flowers are in fact the sexual organs of plants and must therefore correspond to human sexual organs. It is for this reason (some psychologists affirm) that flowers are so frequently made as gifts to those we love—an unconscious sexual act. It is possible to be more precise about the actual significance of flowers by examing the symbolism of their colours.

85   A fifteenth century charm to cause a lover to fulfil his promise:

> Boil a handful of oxeye daisy in a pint of water, and clean the roots of the same. Boil for five minutes to half an hour. Wish for the lover to fulfil his promise before cleaning, during the cleaning, and whilst burning the roots, then pour the contents of the saucepan on a dunghill.

An old spell to enable you to see your entire fate in a dream:

> Make a nosegay of coloured flowers, but only one of each sort in the bunch. Include a sprig of rue, and yarrow of a grave, and find the nosegay up with the hair of your head. Sprinkle it with a few drops of the oil of amber, using only your left hand, then bind the flowers around your head when your retire for the night. Make sure that

your bed has on clean linen. Your fate will be seen by you in your dreams of that night.

Both modern psychologists and ancient oracles **86** alike agree that excrement in dreams relates to money. The theme is found scattered liberally throughout folk stories, myth and superstitions-and indeed the Inca word for gold was 'excrement of the gods'. Freud relates the 'erotic interest' of the child in defecation to the interest he shows as an adult to money, and such a parallel was drawn by Artemidorus in the second century after Christ, so that he interpreted a dream of excrement as a sign of much money to come to the dreamer. A dream of the excrement of animals also implies a financial profit. The proverbial 'constipation' of the miser springs from an image of a man sitting so tightly on his money that it restricts defecation.

To dream of roses in season is a certain token of **87** happiness and success; to dream of these flowers, or indeed of any others, out of season, indicates distress, sickness and disappointments. To the tradesman they forbode bankruptcy and prison; to the married they mean loss of partner.

To dream that you stand in a field of turnips **88** denotes a happy marriage for the dreamer.

To have a great bunch of keys in a dream, and to **89** give them to those who ask for them, is a sign of giving liberty to some captives or being the means of helping the needy.

From a dream of a cradle some do apprehend **90**
The death of a dearly beloved absent friend;
But I must conclude—to believe me you're bound,
That it shortly to you will most useful be found!

91 To dream of food is usually a good sign, but the interpretation will have to take into account what state the food is in, and what is happening to it. For example a dream of eating food usually presages coming joy, whilst a dream of food that has gone bad indicates a loss of money, and not having enough food usually indicates the death of an enemy. On the other hand, certain types of food do not presage good—a dream of vegetables, in particular, is not good, whilst eating eggs in a dream certainly implies loss. According to Birckmayer, eggs represent money, especially hidden money as well as work undertaken, though he agrees that a man who sees many eggs in his dream will soon fall ill. Similarly, if a man dreams that he walks on eggs or breaks eggs, he is certain to be lead into quarrels and disputes. Some dream oracles maintain that to dream of eggs means that a child is on its way, which is probably a simple interpretation of modern psychological theory which maintains that a dream of an egg anounces a new phase of activity. Thus one has to be careful about the nature of one's dream—whether it is just 'food' about which one dreams or about certain types of food, such as 'eggs' or 'bacon' or 'potatoes'.

Among vegetables, cauliflowers are one of the few lucky symbols, for a dream of one brings success in love and prosperity in business.

92 To dream that you are frying food signifies that you will meet up with misfortune, for it betokens quarrelling and envy.

Any root, such as onions, in dreams will foretell,
The discovery of secrets and family quarrel.

To dream that you are eating cheese denotes a large profit coming.

To dream you are eating apples is a good sign. It indicates success in love; but if you only see them, it shows that you will meet with some delay in attaining the object of your wishes.

A dream of meat usually means happiness—though **93** in the traditional oracles it is held that to dream of fried meat will mean that one will be paid well to commit murder! The kind of meat in the dream considerably affects the interpretation: beef indicates an easy life ahead, veal means that you will cheat someone, w'ilst bird meat suggests that you will be receiving money shortly.

To dream of frying bacon presages an unexpected **94** gift, whilst receiving bacon as a gift means some form of compensation will be given to you in the near future. Eating bacon indicates money on the way.

A thirteenth century text reads:

In among the cooks of the land of Devonshire it is said if the rashers of bacon curl up when frying, then a new lover is about to turn up for some one or other of the females of the house.

To dream that you eat an acorn denotes that you will **95** rise gradually to a situation of honour. If you do not eat it, but throw it to the ground in your dream, you will become rich, but another will enjoy your property.

The interpretation of cooking in dreams tends to **96** vary from oracle to oracle. We have already recorded that frying bacon presages well, but a rhythming oracle puts it:

Either roasting or frying, stewing or boiling,
Represents the aproach of evil and turmoiling.

97 A dream of nuts suggests difficulties—especially if one is eating them in the dream. Cracking nuts indicates success in business, however.

A spell to know the fortune of your future husband:

Take a walnut, a hazel-nut and a nutmeg; grate them together and mix with butter and sugar. Mould the mixture into small pills and eat nine before going to bed. The nature of your dream will reveal the profession of your future husband: If you dream of riches, he will be a gentleman; if you dream of white linen, he will be a clergy-man; if you dream of darkness, he will be a lawyer; if a dream is full of noises, he will be a tradesman; and if you dream of thunder and lightening, he will be a soldier or sailor; if it rains in your dream, he will be a servant.

98 Although a dream of cooking beans augurs well for the future, beans under any other circumstance in a dream means great worries ahead. There is a rather grizzly spell involving black beans for making one-self invisible; which is one way to waste good brandy:

This ritual must be started on a Wednesday, be-fore Sunrise, when one must begin by collecting seven beans. Then you must put one of the beans into the mouth of the loose head of a dead man, then two in his eyes, and two in his ears. Then

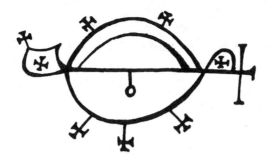

you must draw this character, which is the character of *Morail* upon his head. Afterwards, you must bury the head face upwards, and then for nine days before sunrise you must water it with good brandy. On the eighth of these days Morail will come and say "What wilt thou?", and you must say "I am watering my plant". Then the spirit will say, "Give me the bottle, I desire to water it myself." Refuse to give it to him, whatever he says. Wait until he reaches out his hand to you and you see the secret name of Morail writ upon it, for only then can you be sure that this is not another spirit trying to trick you. When you are satisfied that it is indeed Morail, you may give him the bottle and he will himself water the 'plant' and leave. On the ninth day, when you return you will find that the plant has sprouted bean shoots. Take them and put them in your mouth, and look at yourself in the mirror. If you can see nothing, it is well. Test each of the sprouts, and any which do not make you invisible must be reburied with the head!

A car is, of course, the modern counterpart of the **99** horse and carriage, which in the traditional oracles is associated with the dreamer himself—the carriage is the dreamer's body, the horses his emotions and the driver is his mentality, the thing which gives direction and purpose to the movement of the vehicle. Thus, driving a vehicle in a dream is usually associated with good fortune and honours ('you know where you are going and you have the means of getting there'), and to fall out of a carriage or car means misfortune and illness ahead. The seventh card of the major arcana of the Tarot pack is an attempt to express in graphic terms this very idea. It is not unreasonable to extend these old interpretations into modern times and to see the car engine as the emotions (which should ideally be subject to the control of the driver), the car body as the body of the dreamer, and the driver as the mentality of the dreamer. In this way the dream of the car is a statement of the whole personality and potential of the dreamer, and the conditions under which he is driving or being driven (fast or slow, for instance) what he does (has a crash, runs someone over, or merely drives to a certain destination), should enable one to make a fairly accurate interpretation.

To dream of riding in a coach denotes that the party so dreaming shall love idleness, is given to pride, and shall die a beggar. The dream of coming out of a coach, signifies being degraded from great honour and coming to disgrace upon a criminal account.

To dream you are travelling on a railway is a sure sign of hasty news, but if an accident occurs, it will be of an unpleasant nature.

100 To dream of making a sudden fortune, or of being

very rich if you are poor, is a very bad omen. For tradesmen it means loss in trade, quarrels with creditors, and the loss of liberty. For the lover it denotes that his sweetheart will not return his love.

To dream that you meet with abuse or insult,   **101**
From absolute strangers, some quarrels result,
On business or pastime or money or pleasure,
Yet no litigation occurs from the measure.
To dream you are ruffl'd with anger or passion,
Denotes you have enemies void of compassion;
That a rival you have, who will slander impart,
To sever you from the dear man of your heart.
Should a friend be in anger or rage against you,
Your sweetheart is constant, both faithful and
    true.
Yet anger should care and discretion impose,
Lest danger or sickness, in fact, interpose.

Concerning the dream of being born, Artemidorus   **102** says, "If any one dreams that he comes out of a woman's belly, or is born into the world, he must jedge that this dream is good for him who is poor, for he will have means and friends to maintain him. To him which is rich, this dream signifies that he shall have no rule in the house.

Should a female who's not in the family way,
Dream of having a child, 'tis most lucky they say;
But if she's a maid, let her prudence advance,
Or her chastity stands but a very bad chance!

To dream that you have committed adultery shows   **103** great contentions and debates in your home. To see others committing adultery means the loss of property for the dreamer.

OMENS

Fortune
Telling
by Tea-Leaves
or
Coffee
Grounds

THE idea behind this kind of fortune telling is that the tea leaves or coffee grounds remaining on the sides of the cup make patterns which allow the intution of the clairvoyant to read into the future and present wishes of the subject. In order to prepare a cup for a reading one must first of all drink the coffee or tea almost to the bottom of the cup, ensuring that there are many dregs or leaves left in the remaining liquid. Now the cup must be shaken around so that the sediment swills over the inside of the cup, well up the sides. This must be done three times. Whilst the subject of the reading is doing this he must fix his attention on the question he wants to ask the clairvoyant. When he has swilled the sediment around three times he must turn the cup upside down over a saucer, and then hand the cup to the clairvoyant who will then examine it carefully

The clairvoyant will then make a serious attempt to decipher the tangle of grains into any one of thirty signs, and interpret it accordingly. The following notes about the basic twenty five signs are meant to act as a guide for anyone who wishes to read tealeaves for himself. It is advisable to take the services of a professional medium for serious questions, however.

Roads

When the pattern of tea leaves or coffee dregs make straight or winding lines they indicate paths or ways which the subject will take in the future. If they are jumbled in construction, passing through many tangles much like undergrowth or avalanches in the path, the way will not be easy. If on the contrary they are well marked and clear, the future will be peaceful. Should the way, however formed, end in an abrupt cross line, like the one in plate 1, then the subject will meet with some serious accident or reverse. Whether the road patterns indicate the way through life or an actual journey must be determined from the nature of the question asked by the subject. If the lines are surrounded by specks or dots they are signs of coming gains from a financial point of view.

The star

This sign must be clearly distinguished, resembling one or other of the stars in plate 2. When it is high near the rim of the cup or particularly heavy the sign augurs well for the wishes of the subject. If it is surrounded by dots it means that the financial situation of the subject will be very good in the future. Sometimes the star relates to a child (depending on the nature of the question) and the conditions surrounding the child must be interpreted from the other signs present in the cup.

The lion

This sign actually covers any ferocious looking beast—all the animals reproduced in plate 3 may be read as a 'lion'. Its presence signifies good luck in relationships with people of high quality, or with bosses and the like—new ventures can be undertaken provided it means advancement in theory, for it signifies advancement in practice. It is sometimes held, however, that if the 'lion' is very near the bottom of the cup, or even on the bottom, the undertaking must be put in hand with some caution, as not everything is going well.

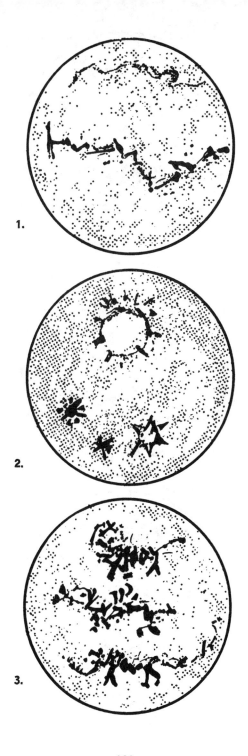

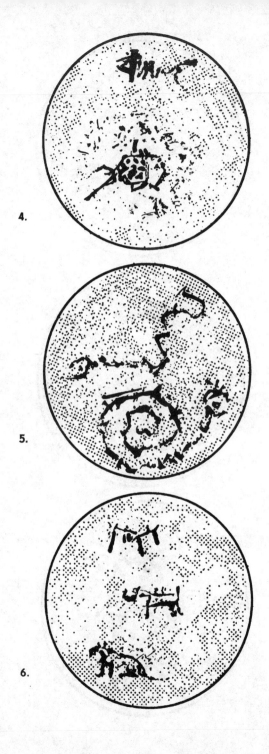

4.

5.

6.

The fish

As might be expected, the fish denotes by its position and condition events governing water—that is either travel by water or affairs of the subject over the water. If the shape of the fish is obstructed, crossed or surrounded by other leaves the conditions for travel or for development abroad are not very good. However, if the fish is clear and unimpeded, these matters will go well. If the fish is surrounded by little dots, as in plate 4, then the subject is called to travel abroad.

The snake

This sign must not be confused with the Road, for its meaning is quite different. It is distinguished by a head, as can be seen from plate 5. The snake is always a sign of enmity or false friendships; if it is near the rim of the cup it promises triumph over enemies, unless it is surrounded by masses of leaves which make its form difficult to discern clearly. At the bottom of the cup it bodes no good, for the enemy with certainly succeed in his evil design.

The dog

Care must be taken to differentiate the dog from the lion—whilst the lion may look fierce, the dog never does, and some idea of its normal form may be seen from plate 6. If it is clearly defined, and near the rim, or at least in the top half of the cup, it is a sign of close friends. If, however, the image is surrounded by many spots and blurs, the friends may not be relied upon. An image of the dog at the bottom of the cup is a sign that envy or jealously will affect the life of the subject in the near future.

The cross

The appearance of the cross always indicates misfortune or adversity, depending both on its size and upon its position. If a small cross (perhaps only two leaves across each other) on any part of the cup side, then the difficulties will be minimal and short. Such a cross on the bottom, though small, is more serious. A large cross near the bottom, or at least below the half way line, means extreme troubles, unless it should be clouded by small dots in which case an end to the troubles will come unexpectedly. The misfortunes will not pass quickly, but they will certainly not be so strong if the large cross is above the central line.

The mountain

This sign, as may be seen from plate 7, is not merely a curved line, for this would in fact be a Road. The whole mass of the mountain must be delineated to have any significance. One single mountain indicates help from people in authority, but several mountains means the reverse. The condition of the 'sky' above the mountain lends a clue to kind of help of reverse to be expected—clouds mean slow depression, storm rain (small specks) mean rapid help, and a clear sky over a single mountain means financial help.

The ring

The ring, provided that it is unbroken, as in plate 8, means marriage; it may refer to an existing marriage or one to come, but it certainly indicates the relationships are the pressing aspect of the question under consideration. If it stands clear in a

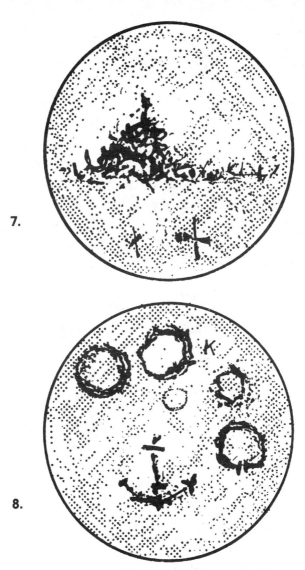

7.

8.

clean part of the cup, with no specks marring the surrounds, it portends a good relationship, but surrounded with specks or large masses of leaves it indicates difficulties ahead. Separation is indicated if the ring is on the bottom, or even near the bottom, of the cup—but if the ring is not on the bottom there is a strong chance of a reconciliation, depending on the nature of the other auspices in the leaves for the same reading.

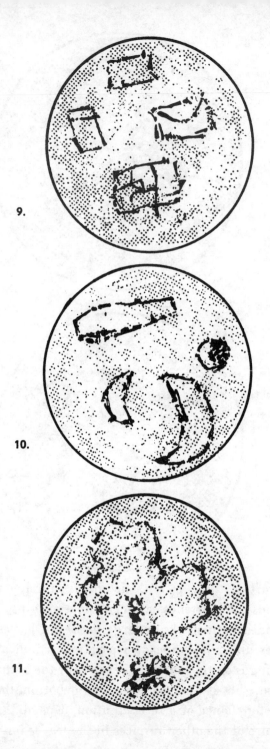

9.

10.

11.

The anchor

This is a sign of a force which keeps the vessel steady during a tempest, and is a very fortunate symbol, especially if some change is expected of the subject at the time of the reading. If it is near the cup rim it relates more particularly to friendships, which, provided the rest of the cup reads well, should be strong and reliable—otherwise, if badly aspected with masses of leaves or with many dots and specks, the love refered to is a temporary thing.

The letter

In its least clear aspect, the letter may be a simple square, as the example at plate 9 suggests. The sign relates to communications between friends, the level and sincerity of which must be determined by studying the meaning of the cup alone. If well surrounded, clearly it denotes good news on the way. If the letter is surrounded with specks of leaves or grounds the good news is of a financial gain, but if the letter is surrounded by masses of black leaves, then there is to be either an accident or a loss.

The coffin

This is the most obvious emblem of death in the whole series of thirty signs. Unless the surrounds be good and clear, in which case a long illness if predicted, the sign indicates death in the family. However, should the coffin be near the top of the cup it means that one will inherit something as a result of a death. Should the same coffin be near the bottom of the cup it denotes that the death may affect the subject, but that there will be no inheritance.

The moon

If this sign (for which see plate 10) appears in a
clear place on the cup, and high near the rim, it
means success in the matter of the question in hand,
but should the moon be surrounded or partly
obscured by dark areas of leaves, the interpretation
must be one of sadness. It is generally held, however,
that the presence of the moon on or near the bottom
of the cup brings fortune in travel.

The cloud

The clouds which so often appear in the leaves or
grounds relate to the desires and aspirations of the
questioner. If the clouds are well formed, clear and
unsullied, then the wishes will be attained, but if the
clouds are ominous and dark, the wishes will be
made in vain. Clouds which are bright will bring
much contentment, whilst those surrounded by spots
will bring success in trade. The higher in the cup
the spots and clouds appear, the better the interpretation may be.

The sun

The sun is very difficult to distinguish from the
ring, and care must be exercised in this direction.
Even so, like the ring, the sun is a fortunate sign for
its presence brings advancement. If the sun is
surrounded by thick clouds there will be much grief
however, though single dots and dashes, as in the
example at plate 8, indicate rapid changes in the
estate of the subject, which will certainly be for the
better.

The bird

The sign of the bird, if unsurrounded by evil countersigns, means that although the subject is at the moment faced with real troubles, they will soon be over. If it is surrounded by a mass of leaves, it predicts a successful journey.

The garden

The garden may resemble a letter, except as the example at plate 9 makes clear, the inside of the square is filled with ordered shapes. The idea is that the garden holds people who are meeting together, and unless there are other indications to the contrary in the same cup, it must be assumed that the meeting together is to the profit of the subject himself.

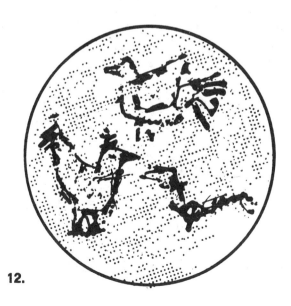

12.

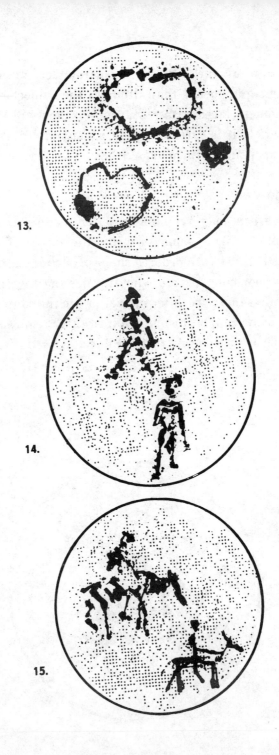

13.

14.

15.

The heart

If the heart stands out clearly, unaspected by other evil signs, it is a sign of coming money—especially if it is surrounded by dots. If there is a letter near the heart which forms the initial this must be taken as refering to the name of the object of the subjects affection. If near these two signs we find a ring, then marriage is clearly in the offing.

Walking man

This image may take several forms, of which two are illustrated at plate 14. The overal impression gained by the sign is one of movement and humanity. The sign relates to a merchant or business man, indicating pleasant news. It is sometimes taken as meaning the return of some lost or missing property.

The rider

Like the previous sign, the image takes on several different forms, but the image is always human and is clearly being carried by some vehicle. It relates to fortune in a foreign country, and to good news from abroad. Coming difficulties or pleasures must be estimated from the position on the cup (the nearer the rim the better) and from the nature of the sky above the rider. Plate 15.

The child

Examples of this sign may be seen in plate 16. When it is not badly aspected by other signs, and particularly when it is near the rim of the cup it speaks well of a relationship with another person which will further the affairs of the subject of the reading.

The lower the sign is in the cup the more dubious the relationship becomes.

The mouse

This is a sign of theft or loss, for the stealthy mouse takes without disturbing, and is rarely caught. If the sign is in a clear part of the cup, however, the subject will find the lost goods once more.

The flower

This sign, especially if it resembles a rose as in the plate 18, is indicative of great success in the arts. It also means that the person for whom the reading is being made will have fine children.

The tree

If only one tree can be seen, and this is well aspected, standing in the clear, points to very good health for the subject, whilst the presence of several trees means that his or her wish will certainly be granted. Specks standing over the trees means that money is on the way, though this will come from a distant source.

People

When people, other then the Walker, the Rider and the Child appear in the leaves these must be interpreted according to the conditions of the subject. If badly surrounded by clouds, jealousy over a person is definitely predicted, but if covered in dots it means that money will be forthcoming from this person. The lower down in the cup the image is found, the less happiness the subject will find in this person.

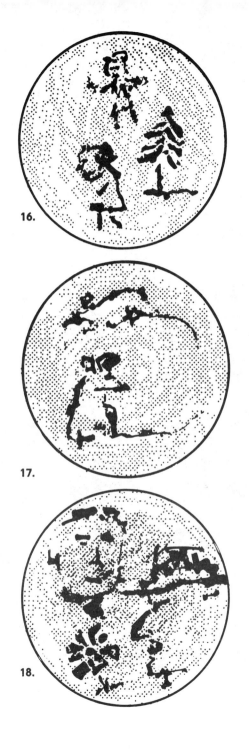

16.

17.

18.

Popular Methods
of Fortune Telling

Dominoes
and Dice
and Cards

THE dominoes must be placed on the table face down, and shuffled well. Three dominoes must be drawn in turn. It is said that there is no point in doing this for any one person more than once in any one month. It is said by some that the dominoes should be shuffled after each one is drawn, and that to draw the same domino twice or three times makes the answer stronger.

1. Means that you will receive a lot of money
2. Means that you will go to a public amusement
3. Means a ride in a car.
4. Means a present of clothing
5. Means a friendly action
6. Means you may suffer from a scandal
7. Means you will move to another house
8. Means a very fortunate business deal
9. Means a visit from a superior
10. Means a party
11. Means a love affair
12. Means a funeral—not of a relative
13. Means you will go drinking
14. Means some false alarm in your own home
15. Means that you must beware of thieves
16. Means you will run into debts and be pursued
17. Means an angry letter from a friend
18. Means a sudden wedding
19. Means bad luck in speculation and gambling
20. Means a great discovery for you
21. Means an illegitimate child
22. Means trouble from a jealous rival
23. Means money difficulties
24. Means that you will make a sudden and un-expected find
25. Means trouble from a quarter you least expect

AN amusing way to find out what will come about for a simple question is to take three dice, cast them, and after adding their totals together read from the following:

3—A nice surprise will be the outcome
4—Not a nice surprise for you
5—Along will come a stranger who will make a friend
6—You will lose something
7—You will not deserve the scandal, but it will come
8—You will deserve the criticism
9—A wedding
10—A christening, which you will attend
11—This death will concern you
12—A letter will be the outcome, and this quickly
13—The outcome will be tears
14—You will have yet another admirer
15—Beware you are not drawn into trouble as a result
16—A pleasant enough journey will come of it
17—You will have dealing with travellers
18—The thing you most desire will happen to you

In the method of divination by cards which is outlined here only the top eight cards of each suit are used, and all those cards below seven are placed on one side whilst the reading is undertaken. Each card has a distinct meaning, which is to some extent affected by the cards placed near to it when a reading is being made. The following notes which set out the traditional meaning of the cards in divination are based on the interpretation made by the famous French cartomancer Mlle. Lenormand, and the traditional gypsy interpretation. It will be seen that certain cards may be dealt 'in reverse', and this affects the meaning of these cards to some extent.

Hearts

Ace — This card means a united household and family. It is also a love letter. In reverse it brings disappointments because of the family, and people who should be avoided.

King — This card means a benevolent man, whose guidance might be sought with good results. In reverse it means a man who will bring unhappiness or disrepute.

Queen — This card means a kind woman who will offer protection and will bring good fortune. In reverse it means a capricious woman it is best to avoid.

Jack — This card means a man who is looking for help in his worldly affairs. He is also a lover. In reverse he is an unhappy lover.

Ten — This card means good fortune. It also means that the seeker is looking for a young woman, or needs a young woman.

Nine — This card brings success, for it is a sign or merit rewarded. In reverse it means troubles which will quickly pass.

Eight — This card means thoughts of a marriage—it also indicates a rival and possible jealousy.

Seven — This card means a visit which will bring contenting news. In reverse it means unpleasant visitors and either boredom or jealousy.

Clubs

Ace — This card means someone will return from a journey, and success in movement. In reverse it means bad news will be received.

King — This card means that you must seek advice from a man and that you must take precautions for a short journey. In reverse it means you will have slight troubles to add to your burden.

Queen — This card is a woman of a gay but dubious character who is being affectionate or flirtatious. In reverse it means a woman who is difficult or openly wicked.

Jack — This card means that you will not gain your desire without effort or cunning. In reverse it is an indication that your luck may change.

Ten — This card brings good luck as a whole, but there will be a small and unexpected reverse.

Nine — This card means either a legacy or a required loan. In reverse it brings obstacles to obtaining a loan.

Eight — This card means a wish concerning a marriage which will bring good fortune.

Seven — This card brings success with money, but means that one should be wary of a certain man. In reverse it brings loss in matters of money and love.

Diamonds

Ace — A letter from a loved one it meant by this card, and in certain cases it can mean an offer of marriage. In revers it means either a removal or a disappointment due to some indiscretion.

King   – This card means that a man scarcely known to you will help you. In reverse it is a warning to be wary of deceit.

Queen – This card means a woman who gets what she wants. It also means malicious gossip. In reverse it means a woman who is a flirt.

Jack   – This card means an undertaking which must be carried out. It also means something which is undone. In reverse it means mischief will be brought about by a man.

Ten   – This card means preparation must be made for a journey—even a journey which is not liked.

Nine   – This card means news will come soon, and a happy journey will be made. In reverse it suggests difficulties in a journey and family quarrels.

Eight – This card suggests a short affair. It also means that the attempts to become friendly with someone will not succeed.

Seven – This card brings misfortunes and unfriendly criticism. In reverse it also brings scandal and loss of a friend.

Spades

Ace   – This card means a high building, a badly behaved child and some satisfaction in love. In reverse it brings sorrows, and traditionally means death!

King   – This card means badly handled legal matters. In reverse it means lawsuits and impending difficulties.

Queen – This card means widowhood, and a faithful friend. It also means loss of a lover or mistress. In reverse it is a sign of a treacherous woman.

Jack – This card sometimes means a doctor, and sometimes a fair deal resulting in agreement. In reverse it means a deceitful man.

Ten – This card means grief through a loss which may be by theft. It also means someone is trying to steal something from you.

Nine – This card relates to a loss or scandal in the home, due to a woman. In reverse it means the loss of a dear friend.

Eight – This card means an illness—but from the illness will come some good. It means a family in tears. In certain cases it also means the punishment of an enemy.

Seven – This card means a resolution which must be kept to. It also means a change for the worse in matters of love. In reverse it means an accident.

There are many ways of laying out the cards on the table in order to make a reading. The most useful, and the easiest to use, is the one illustrated at page 131. When the enquirer has asked his or her question, one card must be selected by him from the pack of thirty two cards and placed face upwards on the table. This card is called the significator, and

its meaning colours the whole judgement of the reading. From the remaining pack fifteen further cards must be selected at random, and the sixteen left must be placed aside. Shuffle the cards in your hand, then place one to the left of the significator, the next to the right, the third above and the fourth below, thus forming a simple four lined cross. The fifth card is placed over the significator.itself and the whole deal is redone until all the cards are used up.

The reading is done by examining the first group of cards to the left of the significator, and considering these as effects from the past; page 131 shows how to set them out. Next the cards above the significator are spread out and analysed: these relate to the influences which are above the person; the influences hanging over him. The bottom row is, then spread out, and the cards which are below the significator are analysed. It is important to determine whether or not the cards above are stronger than the cards below, for these could 'weigh' the subject down is his attempts 'to get'. The fourth groups of cards, the ones to his significator's right relate to the future and these are examined next. The cards actually placed on the significator's right relate to the future and these are reading, and these must then be interpreted, bearing in mind the conditions which have affected the subject in the past, those which are likely to affect him in the future, and the forces which are weighing him down and lifting him up in his life.

The Tarot Cards

THE Tarot cards have been used for divination for over four hundred years in Europe. As a pack it consists of seventy eight cards, fifty six of which resemble ordinary playing cards to some extent, called the 'minor arcana', and twenty two of which consist of numbered symbolic pictures, each with a rich meaning, the 'major arcana'. Each of these major arcana is illustrated on the following pages. Although some diviners make use of the whole pack of seventy eight cards, it is more usual to use only twenty two of them when answering a simple question concerning the future. Since each card is rich in meaning, and the symbolism of each card is somewhat obscure, it is possible only to indicate the general traditional significance of the major cards. However, even with these limited meanings, it is quite possible to make general interpreta-

LE BATELEUR

tions concerning questions about the future. There are many ways of laying out the cards in response to a question, the simplest is the one outlined as for ordinary playing cards on page 131. It is important to allow the intuition to have a free play when actually examining the five cards laid out in response to a question, for it is claimed by those who specialise in the use of the pack that the spirits actually participate in projecting the future before the diviner through the medium of these strange and powerful images. It is increasingly difficult to purchase the genuine Tarot cards — though there are a flood of poor imitations on the market — it is therefore suggested that anyone who is interested might make his own pack from the ones reproduced here by having the cards photostated from this book and by mounting these stats onto thin white card.

II

LA PAPESSE

III

L'IMPERATRICE

VI

L'AMOVREVX

VII

LE CHARIOT

L'EMPEREUR

LE PAPE

LA·JUSTICE

L'HERMITE

The Juggler This is sometimes seen as an image of the inquirer himself. Alternatively, it can mean a foolish man, or one who intends to decieve.

The Popess This is sometimes seen as an image of the inquirer herself. Alternatively it can mean a woman in the subject's life, but one who intends help.

The Empress This is a symbol of prompt action, initiative and undemanding help for the subject.

The Emperor This card is a symbol of controlled will power and expansive intentions.

The Pope This is a card with a double meaning: it refers to useful and instructive authority, and also to the idea of unexpected external help.

The Lovers This is not to do with marriage, as might be assumed after a superficial acquaintance – the card refers to an important decision which must be made before progress can be made.

The Chariot This card relates to the danger of inner pride. Such pride is usually connected with a time when all may appear to be going well, but when there is a hidden danger – usually a moral problem is emerging.

Justice This card relates to a situation where the decision must be taken to objective arbitration, for the subject is not in a position to decide for himself.

LA ROUE DE FORTUNE

LA FORCE

LE · PENDU

XIIII

TEMPERANCE

XV

LE·DIABLE

XVIII

LA·LUNE

XVIIII

LE·SOLEIL

LA·MAISON·DIEV   L'ETOILE

The Hermit	This card indicates a wise act — usually a move in values in an attempt to come to grips with oneself or the world.
The Wheel of Fortune	This indicates a coming change — the nature of this change can only be determined for the rest of the cards used in the divinatory pattern, but it will be a fundamental change.
Strength	This indicates the need for strength of action and for a firm undertaking — though the motives for such an undertaking must be quite clear and good.
The Hanged Man	This card indicates both inner doubt and uncertainty, from which a new beginning may proceed. This is why it

is a picture of a man in an uncom-
fortable position.

Death   This card does not always indicate
death. It always indicates a fundamen-
tal change, which is why it so often
does relate to death.

Temperance This card indicates a need for mode-
ration, and for the examination of
one's motives.

The Devil   Traditionally this card relates to
great inner strength, and also to sickness. It all appears to depend on which
of the figures in the card the subject
may be identified with.

The House This card indicates both ruin and de-
of God   ception. It is often linked with the
idea of illness as the root of this difficulty.

The Star   This card is a sing of coming good
and inner clarity in the midst of difficulties.

The Moon   The tradition links this card with
danger, enemies, and false friends,
and in all probability the image was
intended to convey the sterility of
hell.

The Sun   This card is diametrically opposed to
the previous card – it brings happi-
ness and creative expansion.

The   This card is a sign of unexpected but
judgement merited change which will affect the
questioner and those around him. The

nature of this change will be indicated by the rest of the card pattern.

The World   This is perhaps the most fortune of all the cards, for it gives a positive response to all questions, and outer success related to inner harmony.

The Fool   This is an image of someone (often the questioner himself) who has lost his way and does not even recognise his own abilities or strengths. The formal pattern as a whole might indicate the direction which may be taken — alternatively yet another question should be put to the major arcana.

MELVIN POWERS SELF-IMPROVEMENT LIBRARY

ASTROLOGY

____ ASTROLOGY: HOW TO CHART YOUR HOROSCOPE *Max Heindel*	5.00
____ ASTROLOGY AND SEXUAL ANALYSIS *Morris C. Goodman*	5.00
____ ASTROLOGY AND YOU *Carroll Righter*	5.00
____ ASTROLOGY MADE EASY *Astarte*	5.00
____ ASTROLOGY, ROMANCE, YOU AND THE STARS *Anthony Norvell*	5.00
____ MY WORLD OF ASTROLOGY *Sydney Omarr*	7.00
____ THOUGHT DIAL *Sydney Omarr*	7.00
____ WHAT THE STARS REVEAL ABOUT THE MEN IN YOUR LIFE *Thelma White*	3.00

BRIDGE

____ BRIDGE BIDDING MADE EASY *Edwin B. Kantar*	10.00
____ BRIDGE CONVENTIONS *Edwin B. Kantar*	10.00
____ COMPETITIVE BIDDING IN MODERN BRIDGE *Edgar Kaplan*	7.00
____ DEFENSIVE BRIDGE PLAY COMPLETE *Edwin B. Kantar*	15.00
____ GAMESMAN BRIDGE—PLAY BETTER WITH KANTAR *Edwin B. Kantar*	5.00
____ HOW TO IMPROVE YOUR BRIDGE *Alfred Sheinwold*	7.00
____ IMPROVING YOUR BIDDING SKILLS *Edwin B. Kantar*	7.00
____ INTRODUCTION TO DECLARER'S PLAY *Edwin B. Kantar*	7.00
____ INTRODUCTION TO DEFENDER'S PLAY *Edwin B. Kantar*	7.00
____ KANTAR FOR THE DEFENSE *Edwin B. Kantar*	7.00
____ KANTAR FOR THE DEFENSE VOLUME 2 *Edwin B. Kantar*	7.00
____ TEST YOUR BRIDGE PLAY *Edwin B. Kantar*	7.00
____ VOLUME 2—TEST YOUR BRIDGE PLAY *Edwin B. Kantar*	7.00
____ WINNING DECLARER PLAY *Dorothy Hayden Truscott*	7.00

BUSINESS, STUDY & REFERENCE

____ BRAINSTORMING *Charles Clark*	7.00
____ CONVERSATION MADE EASY *Elliot Russell*	5.00
____ EXAM SECRET *Dennis B. Jackson*	5.00
____ FIX-IT BOOK *Arthur Symons*	2.00
____ HOW TO DEVELOP A BETTER SPEAKING VOICE *M. Hellier*	4.00
____ HOW TO SAVE 50% ON GAS & CAR EXPENSES *Ken Stansbie*	5.00
____ HOW TO SELF-PUBLISH YOUR BOOK & MAKE IT A BEST SELLER *Melvin Powers*	20.00
____ INCREASE YOUR LEARNING POWER *Geoffrey A. Dudley*	3.00
____ PRACTICAL GUIDE TO BETTER CONCENTRATION *Melvin Powers*	5.00
____ PRACTICAL GUIDE TO PUBLIC SPEAKING *Maurice Forley*	5.00
____ 7 DAYS TO FASTER READING *William S. Schaill*	5.00
____ SONGWRITERS' RHYMING DICTIONARY *Jane Shaw Whitfield*	10.00
____ SPELLING MADE EASY *Lester D. Basch & Dr. Milton Finkelstein*	3.00
____ STUDENT'S GUIDE TO BETTER GRADES *J. A. Rickard*	3.00
____ TEST YOURSELF—FIND YOUR HIDDEN TALENT *Jack Shafer*	3.00
____ YOUR WILL & WHAT TO DO ABOUT IT *Attorney Samuel G. Kling*	5.00

CALLIGRAPHY

____ ADVANCED CALLIGRAPHY *Katherine Jeffares*	7.00
____ CALLIGRAPHY—THE ART OF BEAUTIFUL WRITING *Katherine Jeffares*	7.00
____ CALLIGRAPHY FOR FUN & PROFIT *Anne Leptich & Jacque Evans*	7.00
____ CALLIGRAPHY MADE EASY *Tina Serafini*	7.00

CHESS & CHECKERS

____ BEGINNER'S GUIDE TO WINNING CHESS *Fred Reinfeld*	5.00
____ CHESS IN TEN EASY LESSONS *Larry Evans*	5.00
____ CHESS MADE EASY *Milton L. Hanauer*	5.00
____ CHESS PROBLEMS FOR BEGINNERS *Edited by Fred Reinfeld*	5.00
____ CHESS TACTICS FOR BEGINNERS *Edited by Fred Reinfeld*	5.00

___ HOW TO WIN AT CHECKERS *Fred Reinfeld*		5.00
___ 1001 BRILLIANT WAYS TO CHECKMATE *Fred Reinfeld*		7.00
___ 1001 WINNING CHESS SACRIFICES & COMBINATIONS *Fred Reinfeld*		7.00

COOKERY & HERBS

___ CULPEPER'S HERBAL REMEDIES *Dr. Nicholas Culpeper*	5.00
___ FAST GOURMET COOKBOOK *Poppy Cannon*	2.50
___ HEALING POWER OF HERBS *May Bethel*	5.00
___ HEALING POWER OF NATURAL FOODS *May Bethel*	5.00
___ HERBS FOR HEALTH—HOW TO GROW & USE THEM *Louise Evans Doole*	5.00
___ HOME GARDEN COOKBOOK—DELICIOUS NATURAL FOOD RECIPES *Ken Kraft*	3.00
___ MEATLESS MEAL GUIDE *Tomi Ryan & James H. Ryan, M.D.*	4.00
___ VEGETABLE GARDENING FOR BEGINNERS *Hugh Wiberg*	2.00
___ VEGETABLES FOR TODAY'S GARDENS *R. Milton Carleton*	2.00
___ VEGETARIAN COOKERY *Janet Walker*	7.00
___ VEGETARIAN COOKING MADE EASY & DELECTABLE *Veronica Vezza*	3.00
___ VEGETARIAN DELIGHTS—A HAPPY COOKBOOK FOR HEALTH *K. R. Mehta*	2.00
___ VEGETARIAN GOURMET COOKBOOK *Joyce McKinnel*	3.00

GAMBLING & POKER

___ HOW TO WIN AT DICE GAMES *Skip Frey*	3.00
___ HOW TO WIN AT POKER *Terence Reese & Anthony T. Watkins*	7.00
___ WINNING AT CRAPS *Dr. Lloyd T. Commins*	5.00
___ WINNING AT GIN *Chester Wander & Cy Rice*	3.00
___ WINNING AT POKER—AN EXPERT'S GUIDE *John Archer*	5.00
___ WINNING AT 21—AN EXPERT'S GUIDE *John Archer*	7.00
___ WINNING POKER SYSTEMS *Norman Zadeh*	3.00

HEALTH

___ BEE POLLEN *Lynda Lyngheim & Jack Scagnetti*	3.00
___ COPING WITH ALZHEIMER'S *Rose Oliver, Ph.D. & Francis Bock, Ph.D.*	10.00
___ DR. LINDNER'S POINT SYSTEM FOOD PROGRAM *Peter G. Lindner, M.D.*	2.00
___ HELP YOURSELF TO BETTER SIGHT *Margaret Darst Corbett*	7.00
___ HOW YOU CAN STOP SMOKING PERMANENTLY *Ernest Caldwell*	5.00
___ MIND OVER PLATTER *Peter G. Lindner, M.D.*	5.00
___ NATURE'S WAY TO NUTRITION & VIBRANT HEALTH *Robert J. Scrutton*	3.00
___ NEW CARBOHYDRATE DIET COUNTER *Patti Lopez-Pereira*	2.00
___ REFLEXOLOGY *Dr. Maybelle Segal*	5.00
___ REFLEXOLOGY FOR GOOD HEALTH *Anna Kaye & Don C. Matchan*	7.00
___ 30 DAYS TO BEAUTIFUL LEGS *Dr. Marc Selner*	3.00
___ YOU CAN LEARN TO RELAX *Dr. Samuel Gutwirth*	3.00

HOBBIES

___ BEACHCOMBING FOR BEGINNERS *Norman Hickin*	2.00
___ BLACKSTONE'S MODERN CARD TRICKS *Harry Blackstone*	5.00
___ BLACKSTONE'S SECRETS OF MAGIC *Harry Blackstone*	5.00
___ COIN COLLECTING FOR BEGINNERS *Burton Hobson & Fred Reinfeld*	7.00
___ ENTERTAINING WITH ESP *Tony 'Doc' Shiels*	2.00
___ 400 FASCINATING MAGIC TRICKS YOU CAN DO *Howard Thurston*	7.00
___ HOW I TURN JUNK INTO FUN AND PROFIT *Sari*	3.00
___ HOW TO WRITE A HIT SONG & SELL IT *Tommy Boyce*	7.00
___ JUGGLING MADE EASY *Rudolf Dittrich*	3.00
___ MAGIC FOR ALL AGES *Walter Gibson*	4.00
___ MAGIC MADE EASY *Byron Wels*	2.00
___ STAMP COLLECTING FOR BEGINNERS *Burton Hobson*	3.00

HORSE PLAYER'S WINNING GUIDES

___ BETTING HORSES TO WIN *Les Conklin*	7.00
___ ELIMINATE THE LOSERS *Bob McKnight*	5.00
___ HOW TO PICK WINNING HORSES *Bob McKnight*	5.00

___ HOW TO WIN AT THE RACES *Sam (The Genius) Lewin*	5.00
___ HOW YOU CAN BEAT THE RACES *Jack Kavanaqh*	5.00
___ MAKING MONEY AT THE RACES *David Barr*	5.00
___ PAYDAY AT THE RACES *Les Conklin*	5.00
___ SMART HANDICAPPING MADE EASY *William Bauman*	5.00
___ SUCCESS AT THE HARNESS RACES *Barry Meadow*	5.00

HUMOR

___ HOW TO FLATTEN YOUR TUSH *Coach Marge Reardon*	2.00
___ HOW TO MAKE LOVE TO YOURSELF *Ron Stevens & Joy Grdnic*	3.00
___ JOKE TELLER'S HANDBOOK *Bob Orben*	7.00
___ JOKES FOR ALL OCCASIONS *Al Schock*	5.00
___ 2,000 NEW LAUGHS FOR SPEAKERS *Bob Orben*	7.00
___ 2,400 JOKES TO BRIGHTEN YOUR SPEECHES *Robert Orben*	7.00
___ 2,500 JOKES TO START 'EM LAUGHING *Bob Orben*	7.00

HYPNOTISM

___ ADVANCED TECHNIQUES OF HYPNOSIS *Melvin Powers*	3.00
___ CHILDBIRTH WITH HYPNOSIS *William S. Kroger, M.D.*	5.00
___ HOW TO SOLVE YOUR SEX PROBLEMS WITH SELF-HYPNOSIS *Frank S. Caprio, M.D.*	5.00
___ HOW TO STOP SMOKING THRU SELF-HYPNOSIS *Leslie M. LeCron*	3.00
___ HOW YOU CAN BOWL BETTER USING SELF-HYPNOSIS *Jack Heise*	4.00
___ HOW YOU CAN PLAY BETTER GOLF USING SELF-HYPNOSIS *Jack Heise*	3.00
___ HYPNOSIS AND SELF-HYPNOSIS *Bernard Hollander, M.D.*	5.00
___ HYPNOTISM *(Originally published in 1893) Carl Sextus*	5.00
___ HYPNOTISM MADE EASY *Dr. Ralph Winn*	5.00
___ HYPNOTISM MADE PRACTICAL *Louis Orton*	5.00
___ HYPNOTISM REVEALED *Melvin Powers*	3.00
___ HYPNOTISM TODAY *Leslie LeCron and Jean Bordeaux, Ph.D.*	5.00
___ MODERN HYPNOSIS *Lesley Kuhn & Salvatore Russo, Ph.D.*	5.00
___ NEW CONCEPTS OF HYPNOSIS *Bernard C. Gindes, M.D.*	10.00
___ NEW SELF-HYPNOSIS *Paul Adams*	7.00
___ POST-HYPNOTIC INSTRUCTIONS—SUGGESTIONS FOR THERAPY *Arnold Furst*	5.00
___ PRACTICAL GUIDE TO SELF-HYPNOSIS *Melvin Powers*	3.00
___ PRACTICAL HYPNOTISM *Philip Magonet, M.D.*	3.00
___ SECRETS OF HYPNOTISM *S. J. Van Pelt, M.D.*	5.00
___ SELF-HYPNOSIS—A CONDITIONED-RESPONSE TECHNIQUE *Laurence Sparks*	7.00
___ SELF-HYPNOSIS—ITS THEORY, TECHNIQUE & APPLICATION *Melvin Powers*	3.00
___ THERAPY THROUGH HYPNOSIS *Edited by Raphael H. Rhodes*	5.00

JUDAICA

___ SERVICE OF THE HEART *Evelyn Garfiel, Ph.D.*	7.00
___ STORY OF ISRAEL IN COINS *Jean & Maurice Gould*	2.00
___ STORY OF ISRAEL IN STAMPS *Maxim & Gabriel Shamir*	1.00
___ TONGUE OF THE PROPHETS *Robert St. John*	7.00

JUST FOR WOMEN

___ COSMOPOLITAN'S GUIDE TO MARVELOUS MEN Foreword by *Helen Gurley Brown*	3.00
___ COSMOPOLITAN'S HANG-UP HANDBOOK Foreword by *Helen Gurley Brown*	4.00
___ COSMOPOLITAN'S LOVE BOOK—A GUIDE TO ECSTASY IN BED	7.00
___ COSMOPOLITAN'S NEW ETIQUETTE GUIDE Foreword by *Helen Gurley Brown*	4.00
___ I AM A COMPLEAT WOMAN *Doris Hagopian & Karen O'Connor Sweeney*	3.00
___ JUST FOR WOMEN—A GUIDE TO THE FEMALE BODY *Richard E. Sand, M.D.*	5.00
___ NEW APPROACHES TO SEX IN MARRIAGE *John E. Eichenlaub, M.D.*	3.00
___ SEXUALLY ADEQUATE FEMALE *Frank S. Caprio, M.D.*	3.00
___ SEXUALLY FULFILLED WOMAN *Dr. Rachel Copelan*	5.00

MARRIAGE, SEX & PARENTHOOD

___ ABILITY TO LOVE *Dr. Allan Fromme*	7.00
___ GUIDE TO SUCCESSFUL MARRIAGE *Drs. Albert Ellis & Robert Harper*	7.00
___ HOW TO RAISE AN EMOTIONALLY HEALTHY, HAPPY CHILD *Albert Ellis, Ph.D.*	7.00
___ PARENT SURVIVAL TRAINING *Marvin Silverman, Ed.D. & David Lustig, Ph.D.*	10.00
___ SEX WITHOUT GUILT *Albert Ellis, Ph.D.*	5.00
___ SEXUALLY ADEQUATE MALE *Frank S. Caprio, M.D.*	3.00
___ SEXUALLY FULFILLED MAN *Dr. Rachel Copelan*	5.00
___ STAYING IN LOVE *Dr. Norton F. Kristy*	7.00

MELVIN POWERS' MAIL ORDER LIBRARY

___ HOW TO GET RICH IN MAIL ORDER *Melvin Powers*	20.00
___ HOW TO WRITE A GOOD ADVERTISEMENT *Victor O. Schwab*	20.00
___ MAIL ORDER MADE EASY *J. Frank Brumbaugh*	20.00

METAPHYSICS & OCCULT

___ CONCENTRATION—A GUIDE TO MENTAL MASTERY *Mouni Sadhu*	7.00
___ EXTRA-TERRESTRIAL INTELLIGENCE—THE FIRST ENCOUNTER	6.00
___ FORTUNE TELLING WITH CARDS *P. Foli*	5.00
___ HOW TO INTERPRET DREAMS, OMENS & FORTUNE TELLING SIGNS *Gettings*	5.00
___ HOW TO UNDERSTAND YOUR DREAMS *Geoffrey A. Dudley*	5.00
___ IN DAYS OF GREAT PEACE *Mouni Sadhu*	3.00
___ MAGICIAN—HIS TRAINING AND WORK *W. E. Butler*	5.00
___ MEDITATION *Mouni Sadhu*	7.00
___ MODERN NUMEROLOGY *Morris C. Goodman*	5.00
___ NUMEROLOGY—ITS FACTS AND SECRETS *Ariel Yvon Taylor*	5.00
___ NUMEROLOGY MADE EASY *W. Mykian*	5.00
___ PALMISTRY MADE EASY *Fred Gettings*	5.00
___ PALMISTRY MADE PRACTICAL *Elizabeth Daniels Squire*	7.00
___ PALMISTRY SECRETS REVEALED *Henry Frith*	4.00
___ PROPHECY IN OUR TIME *Martin Ebon*	2.50
___ SUPERSTITION—ARE YOU SUPERSTITIOUS? *Eric Maple*	2.00
___ TAROT *Mouni Sadhu*	10.00
___ TAROT OF THE BOHEMIANS *Papus*	7.00
___ WAYS TO SELF-REALIZATION *Mouni Sadhu*	7.00
___ WITCHCRAFT, MAGIC & OCCULTISM—A FASCINATING HISTORY *W. B. Crow*	7.00
___ WITCHCRAFT—THE SIXTH SENSE *Justine Glass*	7.00

RECOVERY

___ KNIGHT IN RUSTY ARMOR *Robert Fisher*	5.00
___ KNIGHT IN RUSTY ARMOR *Robert Fisher (Hard cover edition)*	10.00

SELF-HELP & INSPIRATIONAL

___ CHARISMA—HOW TO GET "THAT SPECIAL MAGIC" *Marcia Grad*	7.00
___ DAILY POWER FOR JOYFUL LIVING *Dr. Donald Curtis*	7.00
___ DYNAMIC THINKING *Melvin Powers*	5.00
___ GREATEST POWER IN THE UNIVERSE *U. S. Andersen*	7.00
___ GROW RICH WHILE YOU SLEEP *Ben Sweetland*	7.00
___ GROW RICH WITH YOUR MILLION DOLLAR MIND *Brian Adams*	7.00
___ GROWTH THROUGH REASON *Albert Ellis, Ph.D.*	7.00
___ GUIDE TO PERSONAL HAPPINESS *Albert Ellis, Ph.D. & Irving Becker, Ed.D.*	7.00
___ HANDWRITING ANALYSIS MADE EASY *John Marley*	7.00
___ HANDWRITING TELLS *Nadya Olyanova*	7.00
___ HOW TO ATTRACT GOOD LUCK *A.H.Z. Carr*	7.00
___ HOW TO DEVELOP A WINNING PERSONALITY *Martin Panzer*	7.00
___ HOW TO DEVELOP AN EXCEPTIONAL MEMORY *Young & Gibson*	7.00
___ HOW TO LIVE WITH A NEUROTIC *Albert Ellis, Ph.D.*	7.00
___ HOW TO OVERCOME YOUR FEARS *M. P. Leahy, M.D.*	3.00
___ HOW TO SUCCEED *Brian Adams*	7.00
___ HUMAN PROBLEMS & HOW TO SOLVE THEM *Dr. Donald Curtis*	5.00
___ I CAN *Ben Sweetland*	7.00

___ I WILL *Ben Sweetland*	7.00
___ KNIGHT IN RUSTY ARMOR *Robert Fisher*	5.00
___ KNIGHT IN RUSTY ARMOR *Robert Fisher (Hard cover edition)*	10.00
___ LEFT-HANDED PEOPLE *Michael Barsley*	5.00
___ MAGIC IN YOUR MIND *U.S. Andersen*	10.00
___ MAGIC OF THINKING SUCCESS *Dr. David J. Schwartz*	7.00
___ MAGIC POWER OF YOUR MIND *Walter M. Germain*	7.00
___ MENTAL POWER THROUGH SLEEP SUGGESTION *Melvin Powers*	3.00
___ NEVER UNDERESTIMATE THE SELLING POWER OF A WOMAN *Dottie Walters*	7.00
___ NEW GUIDE TO RATIONAL LIVING *Albert Ellis, Ph.D. & R. Harper, Ph.D.*	7.00
___ PSYCHO-CYBERNETICS *Maxwell Maltz, M.D.*	7.00
___ PSYCHOLOGY OF HANDWRITING *Nadya Olyanova*	7.00
___ SALES CYBERNETICS *Brian Adams*	7.00
___ SCIENCE OF MIND IN DAILY LIVING *Dr. Donald Curtis*	7.00
___ SECRET OF SECRETS *U.S. Andersen*	7.00
___ SECRET POWER OF THE PYRAMIDS *U. S. Andersen*	7.00
___ SELF-THERAPY FOR THE STUTTERER *Malcolm Frazer*	3.00
___ SUCCESS-CYBERNETICS *U. S. Andersen*	7.00
___ 10 DAYS TO A GREAT NEW LIFE *William E. Edwards*	3.00
___ THINK AND GROW RICH *Napoleon Hill*	7.00
___ THREE MAGIC WORDS *U. S. Andersen*	7.00
___ TREASURY OF COMFORT *Edited by Rabbi Sidney Greenberg*	10.00
___ TREASURY OF THE ART OF LIVING *Sidney S. Greenberg*	7.00
___ WHAT YOUR HANDWRITING REVEALS *Albert E. Hughes*	4.00
___ YOUR SUBCONSCIOUS POWER *Charles M. Simmons*	7.00
___ YOUR THOUGHTS CAN CHANGE YOUR LIFE *Dr. Donald Curtis*	7.00

SPORTS

___ BICYCLING FOR FUN AND GOOD HEALTH *Kenneth E. Luther*	2.00
___ BILLIARDS—POCKET • CAROM • THREE CUSHION *Clive Cottingham, Jr.*	5.00
___ COMPLETE GUIDE TO FISHING *Vlad Evanoff*	2.00
___ HOW TO IMPROVE YOUR RACQUETBALL *Lubarsky, Kaufman & Scagnetti*	5.00
___ HOW TO WIN AT POCKET BILLIARDS *Edward D. Knuchell*	7.00
___ JOY OF WALKING *Jack Scagnetti*	3.00
___ LEARNING & TEACHING SOCCER SKILLS *Eric Worthington*	3.00
___ MOTORCYCLING FOR BEGINNERS *I.G. Edmonds*	3.00
___ RACQUETBALL FOR WOMEN *Toni Hudson, Jack Scagnetti & Vince Rondone*	3.00
___ RACQUETBALL MADE EASY *Steve Lubarsky, Rod Delson & Jack Scagnetti*	5.00
___ SECRET OF BOWLING STRIKES *Dawson Taylor*	5.00
___ SOCCER—THE GAME & HOW TO PLAY IT *Gary Rosenthal*	7.00
___ STARTING SOCCER *Edward F. Dolan, Jr.*	5.00

TENNIS LOVER'S LIBRARY

___ BEGINNER'S GUIDE TO WINNING TENNIS *Helen Hull Jacobs*	2.00
___ HOW TO BEAT BETTER TENNIS PLAYERS *Loring Fiske*	4.00
___ PSYCH YOURSELF TO BETTER TENNIS *Dr. Walter A. Luszki*	2.00
___ TENNIS FOR BEGINNERS *Dr. H. A. Murray*	2.00
___ TENNIS MADE EASY *Joel Brecheen*	5.00
___ WEEKEND TENNIS—HOW TO HAVE FUN & WIN AT THE SAME TIME *Bill Talbert*	3.00

WILSHIRE PET LIBRARY

___ DOG TRAINING MADE EASY & FUN *John W. Kellogg*	5.00
___ HOW TO BRING UP YOUR PET DOG *Kurt Unkelbach*	2.00
___ HOW TO RAISE & TRAIN YOUR PUPPY *Jeff Griffen*	5.00

The books listed above can be obtained from your book dealer or directly from Melvin Powers. When ordering, please remit $2.00 postage for the first book and 50¢ for each additional book.

Melvin Powers
12015 Sherman Road, No. Hollywood, California 91605